T0328380

Cambridge Elements

Elements in Politics and Communication
edited by
Stuart Soroka
University of Michigan

ECONOMIC NEWS

Antecedents and Effects

Rens Vliegenthart

*Amsterdam School of Communication Research
(ASCoR), University of Amsterdam*

Alyt Damstra

*Amsterdam School of Communication Research
(ASCoR), University of Amsterdam*

Mark Boukes

*Amsterdam School of Communication Research
(ASCoR), University of Amsterdam*

Jeroen Jonkman

*Amsterdam School of Communication Research
(ASCoR), University of Amsterdam*

CAMBRIDGE
UNIVERSITY PRESS

CAMBRIDGE
UNIVERSITY PRESS

University Printing House, Cambridge CB2 8BS, United Kingdom

One Liberty Plaza, 20th Floor, New York, NY 10006, USA

477 Williamstown Road, Port Melbourne, VIC 3207, Australia

314–321, 3rd Floor, Plot 3, Splendor Forum, Jasola District Centre,
New Delhi – 110025, India

79 Anson Road, #06–04/06, Singapore 079906

Cambridge University Press is part of the University of Cambridge.

It furthers the University's mission by disseminating knowledge in the pursuit of
education, learning, and research at the highest international levels of excellence.

www.cambridge.org
Information on this title: www.cambridge.org/9781108948081
DOI: 10.1017/9781108950916

First published 2021

A catalogue record for this publication is available from the British Library.

ISBN 978-1-108-94808-1 Paperback
ISSN 2633-9897 (online)
ISSN 2633-9889 (print)

Economic News

Antecedents and Effects

Elements in Politics and Communication

DOI: 10.1017/9781108950916
First published online: April 2021

Rens Vliegenthart
Amsterdam School of Communication Research (ASCoR),
University of Amsterdam

Alyt Damstra
Amsterdam School of Communication Research (ASCoR),
University of Amsterdam

Mark Boukes
Amsterdam School of Communication Research (ASCoR),
University of Amsterdam

Jeroen Jonkman
Amsterdam School of Communication Research (ASCoR),
University of Amsterdam

Author for correspondence: Rens Vliegenthart, r.vliegenthart@uva.nl

Abstract: In this Element, we provide a concise review of the existing literature on content, antecedents and consequences of economic news coverage. We test and refine prominent assumptions and hypotheses in this area. Relying on communication science theories such as framing, news values and media dependency theories, we first outline and explain how media cover the economy. Additionally, we demonstrate that coverage has a fundamental impact above and beyond the state of the economy, both on economic perceptions and political attitudes of citizens, as well as on political decision makers and media reputation of a wide variety of organizations.

Keywords: news, economy, media effects, journalists, public opinion, consumer confidence, political attitudes

ISBNs: 9781108948081 (PB), 9781108950916 (OC)
ISSNs: 2633-9897 (online), 2633-9889 (print)

Contents

1 Introduction

1.1 Economy and the News

There are no issues so omnipresent in current societies as the economy. Almost all events can be translated in economic terms and we know from extant research that the state of the economy has ramifications on all kind of levels, ranging from individual attitudes and personal well-being to electoral outcomes and policymaking processes (see Van Dalen et al., 2018).

The multifaceted and encompassing nature of the economic issue makes it inherently difficult to grasp. On a personal level, people experience the state of the economy through everyday life experiences; for example, by having more money to spend or by seeing relatives lose their job. On a more aggregate level, an abundance of economic indicators (stock market ratings, inflation, unemployment levels, GDP) is continuously produced. The vast majority of citizens, however, will not rely on those indicators. In fact, in many instances, they are notoriously bad at reproducing the state of the national economy in terms of key indicators, as we will show further on in this Element as well (Section 4). Rather, citizens tend to rely on more general sentiments about the economy, as are reflected in, for example, media coverage, and they base their economic perceptions – but also political attitudes and consumer behavior – on this information. Imagine everyday citizens receiving signals about the economy throughout the day, whether it is through skimming the newspaper in the morning over breakfast, scrolling through their phone during their transit commute to work, or watching television in the evening. It almost goes without saying that all these signals will have some impact on how citizens perceive the state of the economy and will for example affect decisions such as whether or not to buy a new widescreen television now, or to postpone this expenditure to somewhere in the future. It might even exert an influence when deciding who to vote for in the upcoming election.

This reliance on news content is not only true for ordinary citizens, but also holds for politicians and policy makers who are affected by the information produced by journalists as well (Vliegenthart & Damstra, 2019). Thus, media content serves as an important mediator between economic circumstances and economic perceptions and behavior. This content, however, is not a mere reflection of the "real" economy. Journalistic selection processes and media logic result in an incomplete picture at best and an adequate reflection of the economic situation – if possible at all – is unlikely to arise from media coverage.

The importance of the topic, the constellation of personal and mediated experiences, as well as the presence of a range of potential consequences of economic media coverage make it a compelling issue to investigate and to address questions that relate to the nature of news coverage, its antecedents and its consequences. Many have done so and research has produced a plethora of relevant findings. The first aim of this Element is to take stock of those findings that provide interesting insights on media production and effects, and that go well beyond the economic issue. However, much of the existing work is scattered, focusing on single cases and lacking a comparative (either cross-nationally, or between individuals) perspective. Consequently, it fails to account for the conditional and context-dependent nature of the production processes and effects of media coverage. Based on a long-running research project that collected a vast amount of comparative data, we aim to fill this void and complement existing knowledge with the most recent insights into the conditionality of content, causes, and consequences of economic news.

1.2 Antecedents and Consequences at Different Levels

Imagine again this ordinary citizen who encounters a plethora of economic signals. Scholars tend to think about the antecedents and effects of this economic news coverage from either the individual level or from the aggregate level. We consider both approaches to be complementary.

First, on the individual level, we put our imaginary citizen at center stage and trace how the use of media content changes people's economic perceptions, their political preferences, as well as their evaluations of companies. We pay particular attention to economic knowledge as an outcome variable and one that is key in understanding a range of other attitudinal outcomes.

Second, on an aggregate level, we examine how economic news coverage affects economic perceptions as well as politicians' behavior over time and in different countries. This set of studies spans a time interval of up to two decades, offering the opportunity to test media effects on a societal level and assess the degree to which they depend on the broader (country) context.

1.3 Studying Economic News Content

The idea that media content matters requires first of all a clear separation of content features that are worth investigating. The economic news items the everyday citizen encounters can differ a lot in content. Scrutinizing these features and relating them to, for example, changes in economic conditions and perceptions is widely considered to be the most powerful approach to understanding antecedents and consequences of (economic) news coverage (see, e.g., Schuck, Vliegenthart & De Vreese, 2016). When studying economic news coverage, studies most commonly rely on the attention, framing and tone (Scheufele & Tewksbury, 2007). These three features are considered as important elements of communication as each has the potential to influence public opinion: they also are the guiding content features in the empirical work that is presented in this Element.

Attention is the central concept in a rich and ever-growing agenda-setting literature. Attention is a scarce political resource and drawing attention to an issue is a precondition for politicians to actually tackle social problems. Much research has focused on the question of how the media agenda affects both the political and public agenda, by demonstrating that increasing media attention on an issue leads to higher issue salience among the public and in the political realm.

Framing refers to the way issues are presented and which aspects of issues are emphasized (and which not). In the literature, a plethora of different frames, either generic or issue specific, have been identified and investigated. These frames provide insight into how problems are defined and who is blamed for causing them, as well as potential solutions for those problems. In political communication, most framing studies deal with how the media cover certain issues, as well as when and how citizens adopt interpretations that are present in media coverage. We will address those issues here as well.

Finally, we look into the *tone* of communication. The tone is considered an important characteristic of communicative texts and has direct impacts on audience perceptions (Boydstun, Highton & Linn, 2018). Recent evidence from seventeen countries and six continents has convincingly shown that negativity evokes psychophysiological reactions (increasing skin conductance and heart rate) and, thus, clearly attracts the attention of news audiences (Fournier, Soroka & Nir, 2020). We know that in a political context negative information in particular is persuasive and citizens adjust their attitudes and behavior more than to positive information.

1.4 Theoretical Considerations

Theoretically, we build on the idea of the positive-negative asymmetry effect (Baumeister et al., 2001): People tend to be more sensitive to negative information than to – equally strong and equally likely – positive information. This *negativity bias* underlies the selection processes that precede actual coverage as well as the effects this coverage has on individuals' attitudes. Extant research into news production and selection has identified negativity as one of the key factors that determine what issues and events journalists choose to cover. Translated to the economic context, this implies that the news media do not merely reflect economic conditions in their coverage, but that negative developments receive more coverage than positive developments (Soroka, 2006). For example, drops in the price of stocks will receive more coverage than rises with the same number. Additionally, in ambiguous contexts, coverage is likely to highlight negative aspects (Damstra & Boukes, 2021). This journalistic negativity bias comes with real consequences. Research has consistently demonstrated that mass media's coverage of social issues affects the attitudes and political preferences of the public at large, and ordinary citizens, just as journalists, pay more attention to and are more strongly influenced by negative cues than by positive ones (Soroka, 2014). This is a strong psychological mechanism that has a firm empirical foundation. Overall, this double negativity bias translates into assessments that, if based on media coverage, are overly negative.

A second guiding theoretical notion is that of *media dependency*. Media dependency theory assumes that the degree to which individuals are affected by media content depends on their dependence on the news for informational goals (Loges & Ball-Rokeach, 1993). Much of the research so far has focused on (perceived) media dependency as an individual-level characteristic: if people report relying heavily on the media for being informed, one can anticipate larger media effects. This finding is confirmed in a range of different contexts (e.g., health communication, Morton & Duck, 2001), including economic news (Boomgaarden et al., 2011). Here, we argue that dependency is not only an individual-level motivation, but also depends on the larger context in which the individual encounters the news, as well as outlet and issue characteristics. Not all channels are equally important for informational needs, nor does each issue require a similar level of reliance on media. Finally, the outcome variable matters as well. Media information is not equally important for every type of assessment that people make as people rely on information from a wide array of sources, including interpersonal contacts, supplemented with experiences from their everyday lives. In this mix of information and experiences, the importance assigned to content provided by the media varies. For example, media content is most crucial to people in situations in which alternative sources of information are not available. In such contexts, media effects are likely to be strong. Applied to people's economic evaluations, we observe diverging media effects: Because retrospective assessments are colored by personal experience and information from the past, these are less likely to be affected by current media coverage; for prospective assessments, however, one cannot (yet) rely on this past information and will depend more heavily on analyses and forecasts as presented in media coverage. A similar logic can be applied when comparing egotropic (personal) versus sociotropic (societal) assessments. For the first, the everyday citizen can rely on personal experiences and everyday life for information, while the second relies to a larger extent on external sources –

such as the mass media. This yields the expectation that media effects will be stronger for sociotropic compared to egotropic economic evaluations (Damstra, 2019).

In a similar vein, media effects may be contingent on the broader economic context. In the period between 2007 and 2015, most Western countries witnessed an unprecedented economic crisis. This crisis was reflected in high levels of unemployment, a collapsing housing market, profoundly low consumer confidence numbers and the faltering of entire economies. Under these circumstances, people do not need the media to tell them things are bad – they experience the situation each and every day, so the influence of media will be minimal. In those contexts, media dependency is typically low, and the availability of information through interpersonal communication or direct real-life experiences is likely to limit the strength of media effects.

These considerations inspire us to systematically investigate media effects across a range of contexts, channels, issues and outcomes.

1.5 Data

Many of the empirical analyses we present in this Element are based on a research project that focused on the causes, content and consequences of economic coverage funded by the Dutch science foundation NWO (VIDI grant number project no. 016.145.369). It consisted of two subprojects with related data collection efforts.

We begin with an in-depth case study of the Netherlands. The data consists of four elements. First, a longitudinal, automated content analyses of the main Dutch national newspapers for the period 2007–13 to understand the dynamics and changes in framing of the economy with a particular attention for the 2007–8 economic crisis. Second, a three-wave panel survey, combined with manual content analysis of offline and online news coverage in the first half of 2015, was conducted. We collected all coverage published by twenty-three different media outlets and analyzed a wide range of content features. Media content features and an extensive set of survey questions about news media use were combined in order to create individualized media scores, reflecting the specific content that an individual had consumed. Additionally, we conducted an experiment among a large group of Dutch citizens to further understand and replicate the effects of different content features (tone, issue and level of uncertainty) on economic assessments. Finally, twelve Dutch economic journalists were interviewed to unravel the roots of the omnipresent negativity bias, as well as the structural constraints shaping news production processes. Overall, these various studies provide an in-depth and comprehensive account of economic news production and effects in a single-country context. While this single-country context might limit the generalizability, it is important to emphasize both that the Netherlands has a media and political system that is comparable to many other Western European countries and that the degree to which the country was affected by the economic crisis was not unique (see more on this Section 5). Throughout this Element, we compare our findings to those from other (e.g., Anglo-Saxon) contexts and find remarkable similarities.

The second subproject brings a cross-national perspective to the fore. It addresses the impact of negative economic coverage on economic perceptions, as well as on parliamentary behavior, and investigates how the economic context moderates the impact of economic news coverage in a longitudinal, aggregate level perspective. Here, we rely on national newspapers, international press agencies and parliamentary archives. Additionally, we employ existing consumer confidence data from *Eurostat*. This is a comparable, standardized measurement on a monthly basis, making cross-national time-series analysis a viable option.

In the various sections, we report more in detail about the operationalization of our key variables and the conducted analyses.

1.6 Outline of the Element

The individual sections serve as building blocks of a comprehensive story that tells how economic news coverage comes about, how its content varies over time and across contexts and what effects it has on both citizens and politicians. Section 2 focuses on the content of economic news coverage and provides a descriptive account of how economic issues are framed in the Netherlands and beyond. It demonstrates the presence of a negativity bias in coverage, as well as a limited variation in framing, even in times of high economic uncertainty and volatility. Section 3 devotes attention to potential explanations of variation in this coverage and focuses on the antecedents that affect content features, most prominently, tone and framing, in economic coverage. It argues that journalists are mainly driven by commercial considerations and often lack expertise to bring the complexity of many economic issues to the fore. In Section 4, we focus on the effects of economic news, providing an overview of previous work and presenting empirical analyses in which news effects on economic knowledge are assessed. We find tentative evidence that more dramatic news coverage could distract citizens from correct interpretations of economic developments. Section 5 addresses the consequences of media coverage for politics, as we explore media effects on the communicative behavior of members of national parliaments. Increased negative economic coverage also yields more parliamentary questions of that nature, and this is felt more strongly in countries that are less severely affected by the crisis. In those countries that are affected more strongly, this coverage has a larger impact when unemployment levels also rise. Section 6 addresses how the public reputations of companies are affected by economic news coverage: we see that negative news can impact reputation, but also that effect is smaller when companies have a good reputation in the first place. Finally, Section 7 brings new forms of communication into the equation, and deals in particular with social media and satire. It looks into the question of how those alternative sources of economic information can foster (or harm) economic knowledge and demonstrates that both satire and, in particular, Twitter can contribute to knowledge acquisition.

2 Content of Economic News Coverage
2.1 Introduction

It goes without saying that the content of economic news is related to the actual state of the economy: if the economy is doing well, journalists will report about it; if the economy is going down, they also will tell us so. In other words: content depends on context, as one would expect. However, extant research also indicates that economic news coverage is subject to some structural biases and that, as a result, the content cannot be considered a truthful reflection of economic reality. In this section, we focus on the content of news, and how this is shaped – or skewed – by two recurring features. First, we look into the *negativity bias* in economic news coverage. Negativity is an important news factor (Eilders, 2002) and news coverage on any kind of issue tends to focus more heavily on negative developments and aspects of issues and events, with the economy not being an exception. The second aspect is *limited frame variation*: much of the news focuses on (societal) problems and questions related to both causes of those problems and potential solutions. Economic problems and crises can be discussed in multiple ways, but the variation turns out to be relatively limited, with a minimum of coverage that challenges the fundamental principles of the current neoliberal foundations of Western economies. We start this section with discussing the central content characteristics of economic news coverage: attention, tone and framing.

2.2 Analyzing Media Coverage

Scholars studying media coverage rely on a variety of approaches, with (quantitative) content analyses being the most dominant one. In these analyses, a range of content features are included, such as *issue attention*, *tone* and *framing*. These features can be considered the building blocks of current media effects paradigms, such as agenda setting, priming and framing (Scheufele & Tewksbury, 2007), which we will discuss more elaborately in Sections 4, 5 and 6.

Issue attention is embedded in the agenda-setting tradition, which assumes that – irrespective of how a topic is covered – the mere attention that media devote to that issue is worthy to consider (McCombs & Shaw, 1972, see also Baumgartner & Jones, 2010). The economy in general, and more specific economic subthemes such as unemployment, inflation and the financial performances of corporations, have a high position on the news agenda of any country in the world. However, temporal variation is often large, with economic dips coinciding with increases in overall attention for the issue (Damstra & Boukes, 2021).

A second element that is frequently considered is the *tone*, or valence, of the news coverage. In many studies, the tone of news is measured by means of the frequency of references to negative (or positive) economic developments, such as the number of times the word "recession" is mentioned in the headlines and lead of newspaper articles (see, e.g., Wu et al., 2002). While negative news might be captured in an adequate way using a relatively simple search string (see also Jonkman, Boukes & Vliegenthart, 2020), positive news is less easy to measure, as are more nuanced evaluations of actors or sub-issues (Boukes et al., 2020,). Often, attention and tone are combined in a cumulative score that, for example, indicates the sum of positive articles minus the sum of negative articles over a certain time span, or only the sum of negative ones, such as the previously mentioned recession index.

Framing digs deeper into the substantive content of coverage by addressing the question of how an issue is discussed. It focuses on the causes of a problem and who can be held accountable, as well as the potential solutions and who can be held responsible for delivering these (Entman, 1993; Snow, Vliegenthart & Corrigall-Brown, 2007). In the context of economic downturns and crises, this framing is highly relevant to consider, as it might have a serious impact on the way citizens perceive the economic problems and use those perceptions to, for example, adjust their purchasing behavior, or their evaluations of the government (Damstra, Boukes & Vliegenthart, 2021; see also Section 4).

2.3 Negativity Bias: An Amplified Response to Negative Information

As discussed in Section 1, one of the most persistent findings in the economic news literature is that of a negativity bias – the tendency of individuals to be most attracted to and most strongly affected by negative information (Damstra & Boukes, 2021; Soroka, 2014). This effect turns out to be strongly persistent in a wide variety of contexts (e.g., Boydstun, Ledgerwood & Sparks, 2019). In most instances, this psychological mechanism is used to account for the differential impact of negative and positive coverage on attitudes and behavior of news consumers. But also on the news selection and production side, a negativity bias is likely to be prevalent (Soroka et al., 2018). Editors and journalists are humans and will by nature respond more swiftly to negative signals than to positive ones. This asymmetric responsiveness is likely to be institutionalized by the knowledge that their readers or viewers will act similarly, leading to larger audiences when the news is bad. It is not for nothing that negativity is identified as one of the most important news values, or factors, in journalism research (Galtung & Ruge, 1965). An additional explanation for the prevalence of negative news might relate to the "watchdog" role often assigned to journalists. Holding those in power accountable implies a focus on the things that do not go well. We will discuss the mechanisms and journalists' perceptions of negativity bias more elaborately in Section 3. The wide availability of "real world cues" – that is, economic indicators that are regularly and systematically measured in a variety of countries – offers ample opportunity to empirically test this negativity bias. A relatively straightforward empirical assessment is to see whether coverage is more strongly affected by negative economic developments (i.e., rising unemployment figures) than by positive economic developments. We present such an analysis in the empirical section that follows.

2.4 Limited Frame Variation

In our highly digitalized 24/7 media environments, unexpected and high-impact events are translated into news content in the blink of an eye. An example of such an event is the collapse of US bank Lehman Brothers in 2008, which attracted vast amounts of coverage worldwide and is considered a key event in the evolvement of the worldwide economic crisis.

A key question in the first weeks following the collapse is what caused the event to occur – a focus on diagnostic framing (Snow et al., 2007; Van der Meer et al., 2014). It is common that, initially, a wide variety of interpretations, which differ substantially in scope, are present. In the case of Lehman Brothers, for example, diagnoses could refer to individual decisions of the board, the quickly worsening economic situation of many US citizens that made it increasingly difficult to pay their mortgages and debts to the bank, or fundamental shortcomings of the global financial system. Also, potential solutions become part of the coverage. Obviously, solutions are related to the problem definition in a logical manner, though, more often than one would expect, there might be a disconnect between the two (Kroon et al., 2016). Possible solutions (prognoses) related to the Lehman Brothers case ranged from replacing the company's board to overthrowing the capitalist market system.

The variety of frames present in media coverage of economy-related events are an interesting indicator of the pluralism of news content. It provides insight into the degree of debate between journalists and key actors in society, which will be reflected in different, contesting frames. Research on a variety of issues and events has demonstrated that, in many instances, frame variation is rather and that frames in mainstream media are often in line with those that hold (institutional) power (Snow et al., 2007). The idea of "indexing" might provide an explanation here: journalists tend to turn to sources that hold (institutional) power (Bennett, 1990). Views and opinions on political and public-policy issues that are absent within elite debates are often absent in media coverage as well. Those actors that have most formal power will find their framing of the crisis in coverage to be most salient. Additionally, the complexity of economic and financial news might hinder journalists in providing a more elaborate and critical account of events and developments. We will discuss this issue more elaborately in Section 3.

It is of particular interest to investigate the level of frame variation in the context of the 2008 economic crisis and subsequent events that had a fundamental impact on the lives of many citizens around the world and threatened fundamental economic arrangements, such as the monetary union in Europe. Additionally, noninstitutional actors were clearly visible in the public realm, such as the Occupy movement that organized large-scale public protest events across the world. In such a context, one might expect to find high levels of contestation and frame competition, with also more radical interpretations present in the public realm. In that sense, the economic crisis offers a "most likely case" for strong frame variation and the presence of more radical and critical frames challenging the neoliberal status quo.

2.5 Approach

2.5.1 Testing Negativity Bias

We test the presence of negativity bias using a longitudinal comparative dataset. For this dataset, we have collected negative economic coverage by international news agency coverage for all twenty-eight European Union member states for the period 2005–17. More specifically, we use a simple search string that indicates the discussion of negative economic developments and combine this search string with each of the EU's country names. We use LexisNexis to collect news items from renowned news agencies AFP (*Agence France-Presse*), originating in France, and AP (*Associated Press*), originally from the United States; both are among the largest and most frequently used worldwide. The number of items is aggregated to a monthly level for each country separately, thus providing a salience-based measurement of tone.

A validation check for four of those countries (Netherlands, Germany, France and Spain) suggests that this international news agency coverage correlates highly with domestic newspaper coverage. The advantage of this approach is that it allows for a comparison that includes a wide range of countries for which negative economic attention is measured. For many of those countries, access to newspaper archives is not self-evident and sometimes even impossible. We have used this dataset to establish the effects of media coverage on consumer confidence and the context dependency of those effects (Jonkman, Boukes & Vliegenthart, 2020). Here, we use news agency coverage as the dependent variable and assess how it is influenced by positive and negative changes in the economic condition and more specifically to changes in unemployment. The latter has been demonstrated to be a good proxy of changes in a country's economic condition and functions for journalists as important economic information (Vliegenthart & Damstra, 2019). We rely on the seasonal adjusted monthly measures of *Eurostat* for each of the EU countries. We first establish whether changes in unemployment indeed affect negative economic coverage and expect increasing levels of unemployment to yield more negative economic coverage. In a second step, we split the unemployment variable into two separate variables, one that captures positive changes (setting negative changes to 0) and one that captures (absolute) negative changes (setting positive changes to 0). If, indeed, news selection is driven by negative signals more than positive signals, the increases in attention caused by negative changes should be larger than the decreases caused by positive changes.

We estimate a basic, conservative pooled time-series model, with months nested in countries. We account for autocorrelation by including a lagged dependent variable and for country-level heterogeneity by including fixed effects. These fixed effects remove all cross-sectional variation, which means that the model focuses on over-time variation within the countries. The unemployment variables are also lagged one month.

2.5.2 Testing Frame Variation

For the test of frame variation, we use a different dataset. Here, we rely on a manual content analysis of the economic crisis in three Dutch national newspapers in the period 2007–13, thus including all the major events of the economic crisis, starting with the US subprime crisis and covering the final stage of the Euro crisis as well. Selected newspapers include the most widely read popular newspaper *de Telegraaf*, the most-read quality newspaper *de Volkskrant* and the financial broadsheet *het Financieele Dagblad*. We selected all newspaper articles that contained a reference to the economic crisis or one of its aspects in the headline. The total number of articles that we collected was 4,258 articles. A selection of 180 articles (60 for each newspaper) was qualitatively analyzed on the discussion of causes and/or solutions of the economic crisis. Based on this analysis, we identified five different frames. These are the *business* frame, the *financial* frame, the *individual* frame, the *Eurozone* frame and the *moral system* frame.

The business frame focuses mainly on the consequences of the crisis for the financial or economic position of companies and attributes considerable agency to those companies themselves to deal with the difficulties they face due to the crisis. The financial frame puts emphasis on the financial roots of the crisis, in particular relating to banks and, most notably, their complex financial products. The individual frame has the consequences of the crisis for individual citizens as its most dominant feature (e.g., job loss and the need to save money). The Eurozone frame addresses the causes of the (South-)European sovereign debt crisis and, among other things, the need for international aid and supranational coordination. Finally, the moral system frame provides a fundamental criticism of current financial and economic constellations. Causes are identified both at a system level (i.e., the financial system is considered to be corrupt) as well as at the individual level (i.e., people are greedy by nature). Solutions are mainly found in a fundamentally different system.

The presence of these frames is assessed for a random sample of 25 percent of all collected newspaper articles ($N = 1,063$). In the results section (Section 4.5), we discuss their presence across outlets and over time, and assess the variation by calculating the Herfindahl index – a measure for entropy that provides an assessment of the amount of concentration on a single frame or a more equal distribution of attention to several frames (see, e.g., John and Jennings, 2010). The Herfindahl is the sum of the squares of the share of each frame in the total framing. The formula reads as follows:

$$I = \sum_{i=1}^{n} M_i^2,$$

where M_i is the share for frame i in the total framing.

2.6 Findings

2.6.1 Negativity Bias

Figure 1 demonstrates the over-time developments in country-averages for negative attention and changes in unemployment rates. We see considerable variation and peaks that largely coincide with important events in the economic crisis – most notably the accumulation of the credit crisis in the fall of 2008 and the Eurocrisis in the second half of 2011. The correlation of 0.73 between the two variables is substantial, indicating that press agency coverage provides a pretty accurate account of the economic situation, with increasing levels of unemployment going hand in hand with higher levels of negative coverage. In a next step, we test whether coverage is indeed responsive to changes in the unemployment rates.

Table 1 (first column) reports the effects of changes in unemployment on negative press agency reports in a fixed effects model with a lagged dependent variable. We see a strong autoregressive process: negative coverage depends to a considerable degree on negative coverage in the previous month. In line with our expectations, increases in unemployment yield more negative coverage in the following month. If unemployment rises 0.1 percent point, on average 1.36 additional news reports will be published during the next

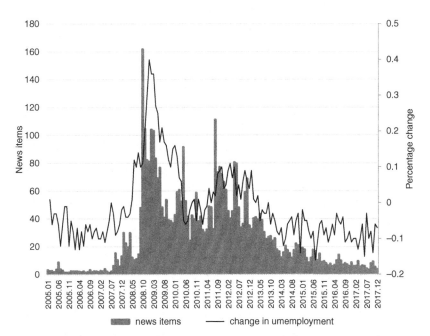

Figure 1 Average number of negative news items and change in unemployment

Table 1 Effects of changes in unemployment on negative economic coverage

	Model 1	**Model 2**
Negative coverage (t–1)	0.77*** (0.01)	0.77***
Δ Unemployment (t–1)	13.55*** (2.14)	
Δ Rise unemployment (t–1)		25.35*** (3.60)
Δ Drop unemployment (t–1)		0.66 (4.09)
Constant	6.40*** (0.56)	4.41*** (0.74)
R squared	0.72	0.72

Note. Fixed effects for countries included, but not displayed; reported are unstandardized coefficients (Bs); *** $p < 0.001$, $N = 4,312$.

month. This finding indicates the responsiveness of media, but to prove the existence of a negativity bias, this responsiveness needs to be larger for negative changes than for positive ones. This is exactly what Model 2 in Table 1 demonstrates: a rise in unemployment (i.e., a negative change of the economic condition) has a substantial and highly significant impact on negative reporting in the following month: a 0.1 percent point increase in unemployment yields 2.54 additional news items. Positive developments (i.e., a drop in unemployment rates) have no significant effect on coverage at all. Thus, negative developments are signaled and selected by journalists, while positive developments are not. This is a clear indication of the presence of a negativity bias in the process of news selection.

2.6.2 Frame Variation

Figure 2 presents the overall presence of various frames in three Dutch newspapers for the period 2007–13. In all three newspapers, the business frame dominates, representing coverage in which the focus is on the consequences of the crisis for corporations. The financial and individual frame receive considerable attention in each newspaper as well. The financial newspaper also pays ample attention to Eurozone-related problems, which were particularly visible during the second half of 2011. In all three newspapers, the moral system frame was used to a very limited degree, with average percentages ranging from 2.5 percent (*Financieele Dagblad*) to 5.7 percent (*de Telegraaf*).

In addition to the restricted attention for more critical frames in the news, the Herfindahl index demonstrates that general framing variation is limited as well. As we deal with five frames in our analyses, the index can range from 0.20 (all frames having an equal share of 20 percent) to 1.00 (a single frame having a 100 percent share of attention). The Herfindahl scores in our case range from

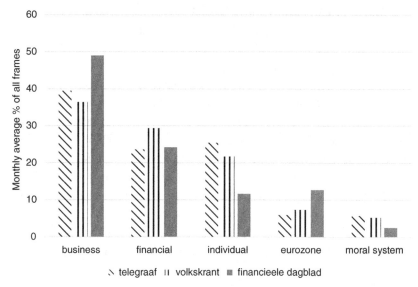

Figure 2 Presence of crisis frames in Dutch national newspapers

0.59 for *de Telegraaf* to 0.62 for *het Financieele Dagblad* and 0.64 for *de Volkskrant*, indicating a considerable level of concentration and thus relatively limited frame variation. We also observe an increasing pattern over time: Frame use becomes more concentrated as the crisis continues, as is demonstrated by a positive and significant correlation of 0.22 between the index and the month of observation.

2.7 Conclusion

This section focused on the content characteristics of economic news coverage. Despite considerable over-time and cross-context variation, two recurring features can be identified. First, a persistent negativity bias, as journalists are more responsive to negative economic developments than to positive ones, which may result in coverage that is more negative than economic conditions legitimize. Second, even under highly uncertain and volatile economic circumstances, the frames used by the news media hardly challenge the economic status quo and variation in framing remains limited. The empirical evidence presented in this section provides ground for further scrutinization. In Section 3, we will unravel the mechanisms that underlie the focus on negativity and the underrepresentation of more critical frames in the news, by asking economic journalists about their working routines. In the subsequent sections, we discuss the effects of coverage, with a particular focus on the impact of (negative) tone on public opinion, politicians and the reputation of companies.

3 Causes of Variation: Journalistic Routines in Mainstream Economic News Production

3.1 Introduction

Shifting from the content of news to the causes of coverage, this section focuses on the mechanisms that drive the production of economic news. We look into the characteristics identified in Section 2: the overrepresentation of negative information and limited frame variation. For both phenomena, we discuss the most common explanations offered in the literature. Afterwards, we present the results of a qualitative interview study with Dutch economic journalists in which we verify the relevance and validity of these explanations by asking whether and to what extent these apply to the daily practice of economic news production. Finally, we discuss the implications of our findings and reflect on the challenges that mainstream economic journalism faces today.

3.2 Explaining Negativity

The overrepresentation of negative information in economic news is well documented: Studies report negativity biases in different types of outlets and across national contexts (e.g., Damstra & Boukes, 2021; Hagen, 2005; Harrington, 1989; Hester & Gibson, 2003; Ju, 2008; Soroka, 2006, 2012, 2014; Soroka, Stecula & Wlezien, 2015; Van Dalen, de Vreese & Albæk, 2017). When it comes to journalistic decision-making processes, one can identify two common approaches in the literature. First, scholars relate the negative content to the profession of journalists. Being the *fourth estate,* the media are tasked with scrutinizing the executive, rendering the government responsive to public preferences (e.g., Kovach & Rosenstiel, 2014). In this view, journalists must act as watchdogs, bringing the news that holds power to account. As a result, coverage tends to be negative as the journalistic profession focuses more on tracing failures than on highlighting successes. In addition, news values theory posits that negativity is one of the criteria by which journalists judge the newsworthiness of information: References to something negative make a story more likely to be selected (e.g., Galtung & Ruge, 1965; Harcup & O'Neill, 2001; see also Section 2). In addition to this *causal* model of newsworthiness in which negativity is considered a feature of an external event, Staab (1990) proposes a *functional* model of newsworthiness. In this view, news values can also be ascribed to an event by journalists themselves to legitimatize their coverage and to sell it to their readership (see also Boukes & Vliegenthart, 2020; Kepplinger & Ehmig, 2006).

Others view the overrepresentation of negative news as a broader phenom-enon related to human nature rather than to the consequence of professional considerations alone. In social psychology, a vast body of literature demon-strates how people, across cultures and professions, tend to be more responsive to negative than to positive information. Rooted in the course of human evolu-tion, people are "wired" to signal negative information, as avoiding bad is more crucial to survival and reproduction than is the pursuit of good. As a result, people assign more weight to negative than to positive information (Baumeister et al., 2001). This positive–negative asymmetry effect is confirmed in numerous settings, such as learning (e.g., Kahneman & Tversky, 1982), memory (e.g., Ohira, Winton & Oyama, 1998), health (e.g., Robinson-Whelen et al., 1997), and is in line with the analyses presented in the previous section. As journalists happen to be human beings as well, it is likely that negative coverage is driven by this positive–negative asymmetry effect instead of being the product of journalistic choices alone. A context of common prosperity may further increase the saliency of negative information. In most developed countries, throughout their lifetimes, people experience more positive than negative events, which makes them, on average, mildly optimistic. Given this somewhat positive point of reference, positive information is considered more trivial as it lies closer to people's expectations whereas negative information appears to be more salient to them (e.g., Sherif & Sherif, 1967; Soroka, 2014), making it more newsworthy.

Finally, there is work that suggests how negativity in the news may be contingent on context. On the outlet level, ideological orientations may play a role. Newspapers or news programs with a clear ideological signature may bring more critical coverage once the incumbent (president, government) is from the opposing political party (e.g., Larcinese, Puglisi & Snyder, 2011). In a different vein, type of outlet may steer the tone of coverage, as Boukes and Vliegenthart (2020) have found that popular and regional newspapers tend to cover the economy more negatively than quality and specialized outlets.

3.3 Explaining Limited Frame Variation

Section 2 identified that frame variation in the coverage of the economic crisis was limited and coverage that fundamentally challenged the existing economic system and underlying power structures was largely absent. The minimal presence of critical perspectives is in line with previous work looking into news coverage of the 2008–9 economic crisis (e.g., Berry, 2016; Manning, 2013; Tambini, 2010; Usher, 2017). In this strand of mostly qualitative research, scholars conclude that financial journalism has been characterized by uncritical reporting in which the dominant neoliberal para-digm is rarely called into question. To understand this lack of diverse and critical viewpoints in the news, the literature offers a number of explanations. Finally, economic news may not only be characterized by a restricted set of frames or perspectives, but a lack of variation might also apply to the topics that receive coverage. Arguably, they do not reflect economic reality in all its diversity. More specifically, some economic issues are considered more newsworthy than others. Fogarty (2005), for example, finds that changes in unemployment rates lead to more economic news (see also previous sec-tion), while changes in inflation rates or ICI (index of coincident indicators) do not lead to more coverage.

First, as markets and products have grown more complex, journalists may simply lack the expertise necessary to fully grasp – and critically cover – the financial world (e.g., Schiffrin, 2015). This puts them in a position of source dependency, as they need to turn to others for information and interpretation (Doyle, 2006). Those "others" are often elite sources closely connected to financial institutions or corporations, as these are typically the ones with access to information and in possession of the much-needed expertise. Being depend-ent on these types of sources does not foster critical coverage in which a diversity of viewpoints is addressed.

Moreover, too much complexity is also an issue given that most journalists serve a lay audience. When content gets too difficult, news consumers may simply drop out. Journalists working for mainstream media, in which economic news is one topic among many more, need to tailor their news products to their audience in terms of comprehensibility. To grasp readers' attention, journalists may select tangible topics that they think are most relevant to the public at large, such as housing prices or pension policies (Doyle, 2006). Thus, the inherent complexity of the economy may hinder critical reporting in two ways: lack of necessary expertise on the side of journalists and subsequent source depend-ency, especially among "generalist" news media employees; and the need to translate complex content into easily accessible and appealing news products for the general audience.

Second, the industry of news production has undergone major changes. With the rise of a high-choice media environment, in which most of the news is consumed online, traditional outlets have been forced to reinvent themselves. Newspapers moved online and face fierce competition from each other as readers are not committed to one specific outlet anymore. These commercial pressures are felt in many newsrooms, and in such a context the structural funding of investigative projects has become rare, because their costs are high and results uncertain (e.g., Doyle, 2006; Strauß, 2019; Tambini, 2010). This may be another factor contributing to limited frame variation as it is investigative journalism that often results in different, critical coverage.

3.4 Validation

While these explanations have been brought to the fore in a variety of studies, only little academic attention has been devoted to the validation of these ideas. In 2018, we conducted a series of in-depth interviews with economic journalists who work for a diverse set of Dutch news media – print, television, online – that reach out to a broad and nonspecialist audience (see also Damstra & de Swert, 2020). Our aim has been to verify whether and to what extent the most common explanations for the negativity bias are indeed valid in the eyes of those who produce the news on a daily basis. In addition, we asked our sample to reflect on the limited frame variation identified in economic news, and to what extent they consider lack of expertise, source dependency, and institutional pressures as possible factors leading to less diverse and critical coverage. The interviewees were selected carefully, covering quality as well as popular outlets. All interviews were conducted face-to-face, lasted about an hour and were transcribed and analyzed using the coding procedure proposed by Corbin and Strauss (2014). A total of twelve journalists were interviewed.

3.4.1 Explaining the Negativity Bias in Economic News

All interviewees acknowledged that their news products tend to be negative. Professional considerations have a part in this, although not so much in terms of checking on power. In most of the interviews, journalists describe how watchdog journalism is difficult to maintain in the realm of the economy. Economic power structures are hard to observe for those who report about it on a daily basis. The economy cannot be reduced to a group of people or a set of institutions: it is a rather abstract force and the diffuse distribution of responsibilities makes it fundamentally different from political power structures. As one journalist working for the public broadcaster put it: "I am not capable of holding economic power to account. I cannot overlook the big picture. I have no idea what is happening in the interstices of high-frequency trading." At the same time, and in line with news values theory, most journalists agree that negativity triggers news selection.

Interestingly, when asked *why* negative information is more salient to them, most journalists point to the temporal dynamics of positive versus negative events. When things go well, there is less to report. Upward trends tend to develop gradually and continuously. But when things go wrong, this tends to happen abruptly, producing shocks and unexpected events. The 24/7 news production machinery – marked by scoops and deadlines – is simply better equipped to capture the latter type of information. As a result, positive developments remain out of sight and news becomes negative.

Distinct from professional roles or values, the general positive-negative asymmetry effect may explain why journalists' news products are better received when the content is negative. Negative news is more salient, provoking more response from news consumers as well as from professional peers. When the economy goes down, the public demand for information and interpretation is stronger than it is during prosperous times. In short, negative news is better received and scores better in terms of clicks and views. Also, for economic journalists to have their stories make the front page (or the eight o'clock news), the content needs to be negative: "I usually write about the stock market, which is the section in the back of the paper. Unless the share prices drop, then my content may end up on the front page," as one of the journalists put it. The better reception may contribute to a general reluctance among journalists to bring news that is predominantly positive. Often, even when the news is good, journalists look for the few negative aspects to balance the tone of coverage, resembling the idea of a functional model of newsworthiness (Staab, 1990).

To explain variation in degrees of negative coverage, outlet-level factors are not considered important. Notwithstanding a long history of political parallelism in the Netherlands, today's media are not affiliated to political parties anymore. All journalists stress the pursuit of balanced coverage, rejecting the idea of favoring one side of the political spectrum. Similarly, the linkage between general tone and type of outlet is not endorsed. While differences in terms of style are beyond discussion, none of the interviewees agreed with the idea of more negativity in popular and regional outlets compared to their qualitative counterparts.

3.4.2 Explaining Limited Frame Variation in Economic News

Lack of expertise and subsequent source dependency are generally agreed upon as factors that may hamper coverage in which a diverse set of (critical) frames is addressed. Most journalists are generalists; they have been trained in journalism and not economics. They acknowledge that such a training comes with less specialized knowledge, especially regarding more technical aspects of the economy. There is general agreement that the economy as a whole, with its multifaceted complexity, cannot be fully grasped. The fact that journalists must rely on sources to get specialized information is not considered problematic by nature. Consulting different sources, preferably with diverging views, serves as the most common strategy to circumvent the risk of becoming a source's mouthpiece. However, journalists agree that different types of sources have different degrees of media access. Academics, politicians, and businesspeople are considered reliable and are frequently used as sources. More reticence exists regarding the use of activist sources, as there is some distrust against the information provided by these groups. As a result, in the words of one of the interviewees, the risk exists that "people putting forward arguments that fall outside the dominant paradigm are less often heard, while these arguments may be worthwhile listening to."

The biggest challenge for journalists who work for mainstream media is the translation of complex information into attractive news products for a nonspecialized audience. Many of the interviewees mention this as the essence of their job, whether they work for print media, television or online news. Even in quality newspapers, complexity is generally discouraged, as one journalist highlights: "We choose not to use any technical terms anymore in order to increase the overall clarity. This may come at the expense of nuance, as we also do not concentrate on details or numbers. However, bringing the news in an accessible way is how we try to make a big group of readers just a little wiser." Apart from avoiding jargon and technical terms, complexity is reduced by the selection of topics. Key to this process is the consideration of pocketbook consequences. The relevance of news is gauged by the degree to which it can be related to people's own financial situation. As a result, media report most about tangible topics such as the labor market, at the expense of more abstract or distant issues. Similarly, because of the *aging* readerships that newspapers face, pension funds receive a lot of attention because this topic is perceived to be "at the heart of readers' interests." Audience recipience is constantly monitored and is a self-standing and important factor in the process of news selection. A lot of page views creates an incentive to bring more news about the same or similar topic(s).

All journalists agree that institutional pressures have increased over the last decade. Especially among those who work for traditional newspapers, a lot has changed. In a context of fierce competition, most newspapers faced several rounds of cutbacks, which have led to a situation in which fewer human resources must produce the same amount of output. In addition, content needs to be delivered in a diversity of formats, at various intervals during the day:

> Previously, you made one story every day. Today, the short story needs to be finished by 7AM, the explanatory story by the end of the day, the big story by the end of the week and the investigative story by the end of the month. You work in four different paces and with a multitude of forms. That makes the journalistic profession much more complicated than it used to be.

As a result of these changing conditions, all economic newspaper journalists emphasize the need to build a distinct profile, by which an outlet may stand out from competitors. For some, mostly qualitative newspapers, investigative journalism has been a means to achieve such a profile. For other, mostly popular outlets, these changing conditions have led to a dismissal of investigative journalism: "You need to be distinctive and at one point, we decided to end our investigative projects and fully invest in digitalization. As an old hand, I had my reservations. Fast journalism is and remains a different line of work."

3.5 Conclusion

The insights shared by economic journalists have helped us to gain a better understanding of the variation in economic news coverage in two important dimensions: the dominance of negative economic news and the low levels of complexity. With regard to the overrepresentation of negative news, most explanatory power is ascribed to the temporal dynamic of negative events, which resembles news values theory in which negativity but also unexpectedness are well-known criteria of newsworthiness. In addition, public recipience plays an important role; negative news is typically better received than positive news, and especially in times of decreasing advertising income and strong(er) commercial considerations, it is important that news coverage attracts a large audience. Furthermore, people are more in need of information and interpretation in times of economic distress, a need that is readily met by journalists who start producing more content, leading to (even) more (negative) coverage when the economy goes down (e.g., Damstra & Boukes, 2021). The pervasiveness of positive-negative asymmetry is probably best explained by its biological origins (Baumeister et al., 2001) combined with a sociocultural context (i.e., journalistic routines) that enhances it instead of being a counterweight.

Regarding the limited frame variation, complexity is key. Journalists are not trained economists and their expertise is limited. However, even more important is the challenging task to deliver news products that are easily accessible and appealing. In our high-choice media environment, audience preferences cannot be neglected. Journalists must produce news that is easy to digest (i.e., not too complex), dealing with the most tangible and consumer-oriented dimensions of the economy, and presented in an attractive format. As a result, complex economic issues that cannot be connected to people's pocketbooks are less often covered and tend to remain out of sight. Investigative, critical news reports still exist, but are mainly restricted to quality newspapers for which these projects have become a strategy to stand out.

4 Effects of News on Economic Perceptions

4.1 Introduction

Research on economic news has been dominated by a focus on its effects. Although the antecedents and content of such news have been studied too (see Sections 2 and 3, and also Boukes & Vliegenthart, 2017; Damstra & Vliegenthart, 2018; Kalogeropoulos, Svensson et al., 2015; Kleinnijenhuis, Schultz & Oegema, 2015), this was often in relation with the effects it may have (e.g., Blood & Phillips, 1995; Damstra & Boukes, 2021; Soroka, 2006; Van Dalen, de Vreese & Albæk, 2017). The interest in the effects of economic news is not surprising given the important societal consequences: Economic news – as mediated through its influence on the public opinion – may have wide-ranging economic (Kellstedt, Linn & Hannah, 2015) and political impacts (Hetherington, 1996).

The impact of (economic) news on political behavior and in particular voting preferences is one key concern in the literature. Elsewhere, we find that economic news coverage indeed affects support for the incumbent government, and that this effect is partly mediated by economic perceptions (Damstra, Boukes & Vliegenthart, 2020). This finding is in line with the economic voting literature that underlines the importance of economic perceptions for political preferences (Duch & Stevenson, 2008).

Another strand of the literature on the effects of economic news concentrated on consumer confidence as the outcome variable. This variable is important in its own right, since it influences consumer behavior, but also because it attracts considerable media attention and many governments take it into account in their decisions about what economic policy to pursue. After summarizing what is known about the effects of economic news, we present a study on the effects of economic messages on the accuracy of people's estimation of economic indicators. This provides an alternative perspective on how well or badly people perceive the economy to perform.

Given the well-documented overrepresentation of negativity in economic news, the public – more responsive to negative than to positive information – may develop economic views that are too pessimistic, especially when negative news is not counterbalanced by positive information received from alternative sources, such as real-life experiences or interpersonal communication. The consequences of such distortions may be real, because we know from the literature that economic perceptions are a key predictor of economic behavior (Ludvigson, 2004; Nguyen & Claus, 2013) and political preferences (Damstra, Boukes & Vliegenthart, 2021; Lewis-Beck & Stegmaier, 2000).

While these consequences are often discussed, not much work has focused on the accuracy of citizens' economic perceptions or how these relate to the news consumed. Especially in the field of economic voting, the implicit assumption is often made that economic perceptions are an accurate reflection of economic reality, setting aside the fact that these perceptions are strongly shaped by information from the media. Previous analyses have demonstrated that, indeed, people's perceptions of the national economy are affected by the news they have consumed, and subsequently drive government support (e.g., Damstra, Boukes & Vliegenthart, 2021). In what follows, our aim is to empirically assess whether exposure to biased economic messages indeed leads to perceptions that are skewed to the negative.

4.2 Economic News and Consumer Confidence

The "economy" is a multisided concept that is both very abstract but may be experienced on a personal level. Hence, the question is how well individual citizens can disentangle what they personally experience in their pocketbooks from what happens on the national level and is reported in the news. The "consumer confidence" construct captures these nuances with survey items asking about people's perceptions of how well or badly the situation of their own household has developed as well as how the situation of the national economy developed (e.g., Kellstedt et al., 2015). These questions are commonly asked both retrospectively (evaluations of the past twelve months) and pro- spectively (predictions of the next twelve months).

Recent research studying the effects on consumer confidence does not exam- ine this concept in general, but distinguishes its specific dimensions (e.g., Boukes, Damstra & Vliegenthart, 2019). The findings of this research have been in line with the media dependency theory framework (Ball-Rokeach, 1985, see also Section 1). It appears that people are most susceptible regarding their evaluations of economic circumstance they have not (or not yet) personally experienced and therefore have to rely on the media to shape their impressions. Accordingly, a distinction can be made on the time dimension: People have already experienced the developments in the past but not those of the future; hence, prospective evaluations will be affected more strongly than retrospective evaluations (Damstra & Boukes, 2021). Moreover, the effects of tone in news are stronger on people's impressions of the national situation than ones related to their personal situation (Boomgaarden et al., 2011). These sociotropic evalu- ations are affected more strongly by the media, because no alternative sources of information are available, such as personal experiences and interpersonal communication (Mutz, 1998). These effects have also been documented on the aggregate level by a cross-national study covering twenty-right EU member states (Jonkman, Boukes & Vliegenthart, 2020), which demonstrates how media effects have been strongest in countries going through the least severe economic downturns, plausibly because citizens were less likely to consciously experience or notice the real-world economic conditions.

Besides these dimensions of consumer confidence (i.e., time and subject) that moderate the effect of economic news, previous work has demonstrated how citizens are particularly susceptible to economic news of a negative tone. A vast body of research shows how negative economic news leads to more pessimistic economic perceptions (e.g., Blood & Phillips, 1995; Doms & Morin, 2004; Hollanders & Vliegenthart, 2011). Research in which a *distinction* is made between positive economic news and negative economic news points toward an asymmetry in public responsiveness: Negative economic information leads to more pessimism, while positive economic information does not cause optimistic views to the same extent (Damstra & Boukes, 2021; Hester & Gibson, 2003; Ju, 2008; Soroka, 2006). Work in behavioral economics describes this psychological process as the "negativity effect," which involves the greater weighting of negative as compared to equally positive information (Ahluwalia, 2002). Because people are, by nature, more loss aversive than they are motivated to pursue gain, negative messages are ascribed more weight in the formation of judgments (Baumeister et al., 2001; Kahneman & Tversky, 1979). We already saw a similar mechanism in journalists' news selection processes (Section 2 and 3), and it is often found to apply to news users as well.

4.3 Economic News and Accuracy of Economic Estimations

From previous research, we know that the way the economy is covered by the media has a bearing on people's economic perceptions, especially relating to (prospective) national economic performance. Building on this work, this section analyzes how economic messages may influence the accuracy of people's estimations of statistical indicators. Whereas the measurement of consumer confidence is rather straightforward (five- or seven-point scale running from *much worse* to *much better*), making accurate estimations of actual statistical indicators requires more cognitive effort from citizens and less is known how such cognitive processes may be affected by the economic information people are exposed to.

Arguably, the estimation of an actual statistical indicator is an equally important and perhaps more theoretically valid measurement of how the sophistication of people's understanding of the economy. While we know that people are able to learn economic facts from the news media (Boukes & Vliegenthart, 2019), and that exposure to economic news increases the cognitive complexity of economic understandings (Boukes et al., forthcoming), the question remains how more or less gentle cues in economic news messages may skew the estimations of indicators, such as the national unemployment rate.

Following the principles of priming theory, we expect that a positive tone in economic messages might lead to overly optimistic perceptions, and vice-versa for a negative tone. However, these effects could be conditional upon at least two factors: topic and message strength. It is still unclear whether a (positive or negative) message dealing with the economy in general influences estimates of the unemployment rate as strongly as a message that has (un)employment as the main topic. On the one hand, people might automatically link these to each other, but it could also be that citizens perceive the two in isolation. If linking takes place, and thus dependency on media to make the assessment increases, it might foster elaboration and thus more adequate assessments, or alternatively yield concern and consequently over-estimation of the numbers.

Another factor that we investigate is message strength: Journalists might either report in a nuanced manner about changes in economic indicators or they could emphasize directional change. Normally, one would expect stronger messages to provoke larger effects; however it could also be that citizens have become used to the dramatic tone in economic news coverage and, therefore, insensitive to the message strength. Altogether, the empirical part of this section investigates how estimates of the unemployment rate are influenced by the interplay between these three factors: tone, message strength and message topic.

4.4 Approach

4.4.1 Sample

To answer this research question, an online survey-embedded experiment was conducted in December 2019. During this time, the Netherlands witnessed modest economic growth, a context in which the general unemployment rate was rather low: 3.2 percent.[1] A sample of 2,600 Dutch citizens were recruited by I&O Research, an ISO-certified research company. Of them, 1,080 people participated (response rate: 42 percent), of which 832 completed the whole questionnaire. Participant ages range from 19 to 64 ($M = 50.72$; $SD = 11.18$); 455 of participants are male (54.69 percent) and 377 are female (45.31 percent). Regarding the highest completed level of education, 11.54 percent of participants have completed lower or vocational training, 46.15 percent are in the category of intermediate or higher vocational training, and 42.13 percent have a bachelor's degree or higher. With regard to ideological orientations, 36.90 percent report

---

[1]   www.cbs.nl/nl-nl/cijfers/detail/80590ned

a left-leaning preference, 44.23 percent report a right-leaning preference, and 18.88 percent identify with the political center.

4.4.2 Procedure and Conditions

After providing informed consent, the 832 participants were randomly assigned to one of eleven conditions. In each of these conditions, participants were asked to estimate the current unemployment rate. But before they did so, they were exposed to a manipulated introductory text in which was mentioned how the current economic situation developed compared to the previous year: the situation had either deteriorated, remained the same, or improved. In one condition, participants were not exposed to an introductory text at all and were just asked to estimate the current unemployment rate (control group). In addition, we manipulated the strength of the tone, resulting in a mildly positive and a strongly positive condition ("economy somewhat improved" versus "economy strongly improved") and a mildly negative and a strongly negative condition ("economy somewhat worsened" versus "economy strongly worsened"). Table 2 provides an overview of the conditions and the number of participants assigned to each of them. Hotelling T-squared analyses were conducted to test whether the groups were evenly distributed in terms of age, gender, education and political orientation, which they indeed were. So, randomization was successful.

Because the item tapping people's impression of the national unemployment rate was asked in an open-ended way, people were allowed to fill in their first association without being steered toward an answer category by the set-up of the

Table 2 Conditions

Condition	Tone	Strength	Topic
1 ($n = 49$)	-	-	-
2 ($n = 61$)	Negative	Mild	Unemployment
3 ($n = 60$)	Negative	Strong	Unemployment
4 ($n = 54$)	Neutral	-	Unemployment
5 ($n = 51$)	Positive	Mild	Unemployment
6 ($n = 59$)	Positive	Strong	Unemployment
7 ($n = 43$)	Negative	Mild	Economy
8 ($n = 55$)	Negative	Strong	Economy
9 ($n = 47$)	Neutral	-	Economy
10 ($n = 60$)	Positive	Mild	Economy
11 ($n = 62$)	Positive	Strong	Economy

survey item. This is a strength of the design, but it also makes the analyses prone to distortion by outliers. We dropped those observations in which the estimated unemployment rate was more than 10 percent points above the actual percentage (i.e., all respondents estimating the unemployment rate to be 13.2 percent or higher, which exceeds the highest rates since World War II), leading to a final sample of 601 observations; estimates above 13.2 percent were deemed unrealistic.

4.5 Results

4.5.1 Descriptive Analyses

Overall, respondents were more pessimistic than economic reality justified. This could partly be due to the very low unemployment rate at the time this study was fielded. Participants in the control group who were not exposed to any economic information estimated, on average, the unemployment rate to be 5.93 percent, which is almost twice as high as the actual rate in December 2019 (3.2 percent). Figure 3 provides an overview of the average estimation per condition, illustrating how the tone of the information matters as does the topic the text deals with. People who were exposed to negative economic information, reported higher estimations of the unemployment rate than those who were exposed to positive economic information, although only when the tone of the content was strong ("economy strongly worsened" versus "economy strongly improved"). When exposed to mildly positive or mildly negative information, the difference in estimations is minimal. Looking at the

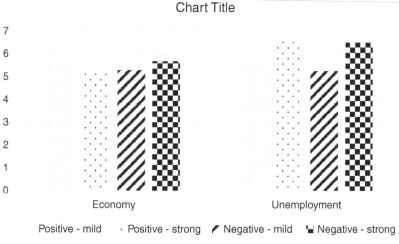

Figure 3 Mean estimations of unemployment rate – per condition

differences across conditions in which information related to unemployment was presented, the pattern is very different. Interestingly, those who were exposed to positive information were more pessimistic about the unemployment rate than those who were exposed to negative information. This could be related to the wording of the items, as the positive condition speaks of *downward* trends and the negative conditions refers to *upward* trends. This is just another example of the difficulty to accurately understand economic matters.

4.5.2 Explaining People's Estimations

We conducted OLS regression analysis to obtain a better understanding of the relative impact that these content features may have had on the accuracy of people's estimations. Our dependent variable was the degree to which people's estimations deviate from the correct unemployment rate (3.2 percent), a score of − 1 indicating an estimate of 2.2 percent, a score of 1 implying an estimate of 4.2 percent and a score of 0 indicating the answer being precisely correct. Table 3 presents the results; note that the control condition is dropped from the analysis to analyze the 5 (tone) × 2 (topic) in a clean manner ($n = 552$). Model 1 estimates the main effect of each information feature. We do not find any effects of the tone of information on the accuracy of people's estimations. This runs counter to what we would expect from a theoretical point of view, but it is in line with the results

Table 3 OLS regression estimating (in)accuracy of estimations national unemployment rate

Variable	Model 1		Model 2	
	B	Beta	b	Beta
Constant	2.33 (0.29)***		2.52 (0.32)***	
Positive information	−0.16 (0.35)	−0.03	0.00 (0.37)	0.00
Negative information	−0.32 (0.35)	−0.06	−0.36 (0.46)	−0.07
Unemployment topic	0.44 (0.30)θ	0.08	0.11 (0.34)	0.02
Strength of tone	0.49 (0.25)θ	0.09	−0.36 (0.42)	−0.07
Negativity * topic			−0.24 (0.48)	−0.04
Negativity * strength			0.65 (0.51)	0.10
Topic * strength			1.04 (0.47)*	0.16
R^2	0.01		0.03	
N	552		552	
AIC	4.827		4.825	

Values are unstandardized beta coefficients with standard errors in parentheses
θ$p < 0.10$, *$p < 0.05$, ** $p < 0.01$, *** $p < 0.001$

displayed in Figure 3, which showed respondents in positive unemployment conditions providing comparatively higher estimations. The topic the information deals with has a positive impact on people's estimates, although the coefficient is only marginally significant ($p = 0.053$). This implies that the estimates made by people who were exposed to information in which the current unemployment rate was discussed, tend to be more distorted (higher deviations from real unemployment rate) than the estimates made by people in the "general economy" condition. In addition, we observe a positive impact of "strength of tone"; when the information is presented in strong wording (economy/unemployment has "strongly improved / strongly worsened"), people tend to report less accurate estimates of the national unemployment rate. Again, this positive impact is marginally significant ($p = 0.052$). Of course, for both effects it is hard to think of mechanisms that take place in which the actual tone of the content does not play a role. As outlined previously, it could well be that the absence of this tone effect is related to the wording of the items, especially in those conditions discussing trends in unemployment rates.

As previous work has demonstrated that content features do not operate in isolation but tend to interact when shaping public opinion (e.g., Damstra, 2019), we add three interaction terms to the equation in a second model. Again, the tone of the content does not have an impact, neither does it moderate the effects of topic or strength of the message.[2] We do observe a positive and significant interaction effect of the topic the information deals with and the strength with which the information is presented. When people are exposed to information dealing with unemployment, the positive effect of the strength of the information becomes stronger, leading to even more distorted estimates of the actual unemployment rate. Although we are reluctant to draw bold conclusions based on a single experiment, the findings suggest that people's knowledge can easily be influenced by related information that is firmly worded.

4.6 Conclusion

The current section shows that not only the well-researched construct of consumer confidence is influenced by media reports, but that economic messages may also influence people's estimates of the unemployment rate. The effects were somewhat surprising as we did not observe any impact of the tone of the content, which could be related to the specific wording of the survey items describing trends in unemployment rates (declining unemployment

---

[2] Note that the same set of analyses is conducted for positive tonality interacting with topic and strength of message, yielding very similar results.

trends actually being positive news, and increasing unemployment implying negative developments). The impact of topic and strength of wording illustrate how information, even in the form of a brief introductory text, may have a bearing on public perceptions. The main effect of topic suggests that the cognitive effort needed to link information about the general economy to estimates of a specific subdimension is considerable. People do not automatically link changes in the general economy to consequences for the nation's unemployment rate. When exposed to information dealing with unemployment, people probably do make this connection; however, it leads to *less* accurate estimates as people think unemployment is even higher (resembling direct issue effects found by Damstra, 2019). In terms of media dependency, one could interpret these findings as indicating that direct relevance (discussing unemployment) might increase attention and concern, and consequently yield overestimations of the size of the problem. Also, the strength of the message decreases the accuracy of estimates. Thus, when journalists use stronger words to describe economic trends, people are less likely to make a correct estimation. More dramatic news coverage could thus distract citizens from correct interpretations of economic developments. The positive interaction between topic and strength points to the conditionality of economic news effects on content-related features. While research has documented the moderating impact of external (economic) contexts (e.g., Jonkman, Boukes & Vliegenthart, 2020; Vliegenthart & Damstra, 2019) and news formats (Boukes & Vliegenthart, 2019), more scholarly attention could be devoted to the conditionality on type of content.

Our dependent variable – accuracy of people's estimations of national unemployment rates – provides an interesting alternative for existing items normally used to test the effects of economic news: asking people's evaluations about economic developments (similar to consumer confidence), but in a way that levels of accuracy can be determined (similar to knowledge studies). This is a more challenging test of economic information effects as there is no predetermined scale of the dependent variable and outliers must be dealt with. However, in contrast to work on political knowledge, the accuracy of people's economic perceptions and their susceptibility to economic information is not often tested empirically. The analyses in this section provide a first step in this direction. It would be interesting to further examine the contingency of news effects by exploring different economic topics next to the ones in our analyses (e.g., inflation, housing prices). As people's economic views are broadly considered a key predictor of various economic and political attitudes, assessing the accuracy of these views deserves more scholarly attention.

5 Economic News Coverage and Political Attention

5.1 Introduction

In this section, we shift the attention from media effects on the public to the political impact that economic coverage might have. The idea that an economic situation may have clear political consequences is beyond discussion. In terms of electoral consequences, a rich literature demonstrates how incumbent parties often are punished for poor economic performances (economic voting literature; see Lewis-Beck & Paldam, 2000). In terms of policy consequences, economic conditions are a strong incentive for governments to make adjustments. In some instances, such as the 2007–8 economic crisis, such reforms are fundamental and have a direct impact on people's daily lives. While effects of media coverage on policy changes and reforms have been documented (Melenhorst, 2015), they are not easy to pinpoint exactly. Many policy changes are the result of long-term and path-dependent processes, and sometimes media coverage plays an initiating or accelerating role while at other times it does not have much of an influence. This is different when it comes to what Walgrave and Van Aelst (2006) label "*symbolic* political agendas". These political agendas cover a range of activities that might not have direct policy consequences, but highlight priorities to the electorate and serve as an instrument in the day-to-day government-controlling function of parliaments. Furthermore, in most instances, problems and issues have to obtain a place on those agendas before they receive more substantial (political) attention (Cobb & Elder, 1971). The political agenda is often measured by means of the questions posed by members of parliaments (MPs) to (members of) the government. There is considerable work that demonstrates how increasing media attention for political issues leads to more parliamentary questions posed on the same issue in the subsequent period. Generally speaking, the impact of media coverage on parliamentary questions is stronger than the other way around (Vliegenthart et al., 2016). MPs use the media as a source of information to learn about issues that are deemed important and require their attention, and they do so in a systematic and strategic way (Van Aelst & Vliegenthart, 2014).

In recent years, a wide range of studies have focused on the moderating factors that determine the presence and size of political agenda-setting effects. These studies, for example, demonstrate that opposition MPs are more strongly affected by media coverage than government MPs (Vliegenthart & Walgrave, 2011), that political parties focus most on the issues they "own" (i.e., have a good reputation on) and that MPs devote most attention to media that are ideologically close (political parallelism; Van der Pas et al., 2017; Vliegenthart & Mena Montes, 2014).

Remarkably, most of the research relies on single-country studies, with only a few studies taking a comparative perspective. Several two-country studies show similar patterns across different countries, or find nuanced differences that are attributed to differences in political and media system features (e.g., Sciarini, Tresch & Vliegenthart, 2020; Vliegenthart & Walgrave, 2011). A study of seven Western European countries demonstrates that this broader context indeed matters (Vliegenthart et al., 2016). Overall, media exert a stronger influence on opposition parties in countries with single-party governments compared to those with multi-party governments. But, for government parties the pattern is reversed.

In this section, we focus on negative economic news coverage and parliamentary questions in four Western European countries. We are interested in knowing whether economic conditions moderate the effect media have on parliament, both in a cross-country, as well as in an over-time perspective. One of the big advantages of studying the economy is the availability of real-world data. Many of the previous studies suffered from potential omitted-variable bias by establishing (causal) relationships between media and political agendas without considering developments and/or trends outside those realms that might affect both.

5.2 Negative Economic Coverage

The focus in this section is on *negative* economic news. This focus on negativity can be legitimized in various ways. First, previous research has shown that negative news in particular affects the political agenda (Thesen, 2013). In line with this finding, Sevenans and Vliegenthart (2016) demonstrate that coverage containing conflict frames, a feature closely related to negativity (Lengauer et al., 2012), is more influential than coverage that does not. Similarly, news in which the government is blamed for economic performances leads to less public support for government policies, while news in which the government receives credit for economic performances, does not have an impact (Damstra, Boukes & Vliegenthart, 2020). Second, parliamentary questions are often problem driven and focus, by nature, on issues that merit attention because they do not go well. Third, a practical advantage of the focus on negative economic coverage is that it is easily captured using a simple set of search terms that have proven highly effective in previous work.

In line with extant research on political agenda setting, our general expectation is that the more attention media devote to negative economic developments, the more parliamentary questions will be asked about this issue. In addition, we want to examine the moderating impact of the economic context in which this interaction between politicians and journalists takes place. We depart from the premise that media content matters less in contexts of economic distress. In those instances, MPs do not need the media to tell them they have to devote attention to economic matters: the issue is completely obtrusive to them (Zucker, 1978) and they will devote ample attention to it irrespective of heightened media attention. Here, we assume that ideas about media dependency apply to MPs in similar ways as they do to ordinary citizens. However, as MPs are elected officials, they must actively communicate that they know of and care about constituents' concerns. If the economic situation worsens, MPs might be even more inclined to follow media content and thus be more strongly affected.

5.3 Approach

We rely on a computer-assisted content analysis of newspaper coverage and parliamentary archives in four Western European countries: Germany, the Netherlands, France and Spain for the period 2005–16 (mid-2006 for Spain due to data availability). This period includes the build-up toward the global economic crisis of 2007–8, as well as its (long) aftermath. While all countries have been affected by the crisis, they were so to different degrees. Economic data demonstrate that in particular Spain, and France to a lesser degree, suffered heavily from the crisis. The consequences in Germany, as well as in the Netherlands, were less severe. Given our interest in differential political agenda-setting effects due to different economic contexts, the analyses presented here are split into two, with France and Spain on the one hand and Germany and the Netherlands on the other.

In each country, we collected the number of articles in one leading newspaper per month that devoted attention to negative economic developments. We did this by employing (translations of) a search string that has been used in previous studies (e.g., Hollanders & Vliegenthart, 2011). The newspapers we considered were *die Welt* for Germany, *NRC Handelsblad* for the Netherlands, *Le Figaro* for France and *El País* for Spain. Parliamentary questions were obtained from the archives of the *Bundestag*, *Tweede Kamer*, *Assemblée Nationale* and the *Congreso de los Diputados*, respectivelty.

To capture the (changing) economic situation, we use the monthly change in unemployment levels, which is a commonly used indicator of the direction the economy is heading. The seasonally adjusted data are obtained from the European Union's statistical office *Eurostat*.

Our dataset has a time-series structure with monthly level data for each of the four countries. We account for this specific data structure in various ways. First, we use lagged values for our independent variables, to meet the basic require-ment of causality that the cause has to precede the consequence. Second, we include a lagged dependent variable as additional independent variable to account for temporal dependency of observations. We include dummy variables (fixed effects) to account for country-level heterogeneity. Additionally, to facilitate cross-country comparison, we standardize the media and parliamen-tary data. More sophisticated time-series models can be used in this specific case, and we actually presented those elsewhere (Vliegenthart & Damstra, 2019), but we opted for accessible and easy-to-interpret ones here. These more advanced models yield highly similar results as those presented in the following.

5.4 Results

For illustrative purposes, Figure 4 provides an overview of newspaper and parliamentary attention for negative economic developments in one of the four countries: Germany.

Figure 4 shows us that media seem to reflect the economic reality, with peaks in attention coinciding with major economic events in 2008 and 2009; the number of parliamentary questions is also at higher levels in those years. Both series correlate substantially, with an r of 0.58. But a strong correlation does not imply causation – we need a more rigid model to assess this. Table 4 presents the results of two time-series models that focus on the main effect of negative economic coverage on political attention. First of all, the results confirm our

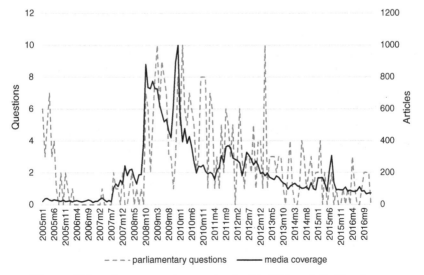

Figure 4 Negative economic attention in *Die Welt* and die Bundestag

Table 4 The effect of media coverage on parliamentary questions

	Severe crisis	No severe crisis
Parliamentary questions (t-1)	0.489*** (0.053)	0.412*** (0.052)
Newspaper articles (t-1)	0.216*** (0.054)	0.387*** (0.052)
Change in unemployment (t-1)	0.690** (0.255)	0.506 (0.471)
Constant	−0.003 (0.060)	0.001 (0.057)
R^2 (N)	0.509 (266)	0.543 (284)

Note. Parliamentary questions and newspaper coverage have been standardized; fixed effects for countries are included (but not displayed). ** $p < 0.01$; *** $p < 0.001$

general expectation that media matter for politics. In both countries with and without a severe crisis, we see that when media devote more attention to negative economic developments, in the subsequent month parliamentarians will do so as well. The effect in the countries with no severe crisis, however, is substantially stronger ($\Delta\beta = 0.171$, SE $= 0.075$, $p < 0.05$). As we anticipated, in those countries where difficult economic circumstances were omnipresent, MPs relied less on media as an inspiration for parliamentary behavior.

Furthermore, Table 4 shows that parliamentary questioning behavior is autoregressive: the attention in the previous month has a considerable influence on parliamentary attention in the current month. Finally, changes in unemployment rates also affect the number of questions asked, with rising unemployment yielding more questions, though this effect is not significant for the countries that are less severely affected by the economic crisis.

The final question we are interested in is whether politicians react (differently) to media in changing economic conditions. Therefore, we replicate the analyses as presented in Table 4 and include an additional interaction between media coverage and changes in unemployment. Table 5 presents the results.

The results demonstrate that in the countries that suffered most from the crisis, (further) worsening economic conditions indeed increase the impact of newspaper coverage on MPs. Thus, while in such a context the general media effect is more limited, it does increase when unemployment figures rise. We do not find such a change in responsiveness in the Germany/Netherlands analysis: here we see that the effect of media on politics is rather stable across changing economic conditions.

5.5 Conclusion

Politicians, and in particular members of parliament, are in the business of representation. One of their key tasks is acting upon societal concerns:

concerns that are often reflected in media content. Our analyses reveal that, across the board, MPs indeed respond to media content. The degree to which they do so depends on the (changing) economic context they act in. Assuming politicians to be strategic actors, they have to weigh a vast amount of information on a day-to-day basis and decide on which incoming signals to respond. In this process, it makes sense that novel and unexpected information stands out and will increase their reliance and dependence on the media. In contexts where economic conditions are poor yet stable, incoming media information is less influential. Only when the situation worsens in such a context, will MPs start to weigh media information more heavily and feel the need to be more responsive.

These findings add to our understanding of political agenda-setting processes, but also broaden our understanding of the consequence of economic news coverage beyond public opinion and consumer behavior. When it comes to politicians, we again find evidence for the importance of context that defines the relevance of incoming information as a moderator of media effects. These findings jibe well with those earlier reported on the importance of media dependency for citizens that is partially determined by the (economic) context they live in.

6 Tone and Its Effects on the Reputation of Firms

6.1 Introduction

News coverage can affect the way citizens think about the economy in several ways (see Section 4). This current section zooms in on the influence of news coverage on citizens' attitudes toward firms. Corporations are important actors in economic news (Kalogeropoulos, Svensson et al., 2015), and media attention to firms has been growing (Graf-Vlachy et al., 2019; Pallas, Strannegård & Jonsson, 2014) in reaction to the ever-increasing influence of corporate power in the economic and political spheres (Scherer, Palazzo & Matten, 2014). One way to account for the attitudinal effects of news on citizens is via the construct of *corporate reputation*, which refers to the overall evaluation of a firm by the general public or expert stakeholders (Meijer & Kleinnijenhuis, 2006a). In the digital age, traditional news media are still important agenda setters for the corporate domain (Vogler & Eisenegger, 2020), because most people keep using the news media as their primary source of information on distant corporate conduct (Graf-Vlachy et al., 2019). News coverage on corporate actors may therefore have significant reputational consequences for economic actors, such as firms.

6.2 News and Corporate Reputation

Several characteristics of news content – like the tone of the coverage – can influence corporate reputation (Meijer & Kleinnijenhuis, 2006a, 2006b; Zhang, 2018). Notably, variation in corporate reputation has been related to business indicators, such as corporate economic performance, employer popularity, and investor attractiveness (e.g., Deephouse, 2000).

Carrol and McCombs (2003) were the first to argue that "the central theoretical idea [of agenda setting] – the transfer of salience from the media agenda to the public agenda – fits equally well in the world of business communication" (p. 36). In line with research in the field of political communication (see, e.g., McCombs, 2005) scholars interested in corporate news have distinguished between first- and second-level agenda setting (e.g., Kiousis, Popescu & Mitrook, 2007; Meijer & Kleinnijenhuis, 2006a, 2006b; Vogler & Eisenegger, 2020; Zhang, 2018). The first level of analysis commonly refers to the salience transfer of corporate actors or issues between the media agenda and the public agenda, while the second level pertains to the transfer of attributes of those objects. The tone related to firms or issues can be considered a relevant example of this second level.

Despite the aforementioned work, agenda-setting research on corporate attitude formation has been relatively limited since Carrol and McCombs' (2003) paper and Meijer and Kleinnijenhuis' (2006a) seminal work, in which a clear relationship between news and reputation was observed. Yet, recent empirical results are still mixed and inconclusive. Reasons for the limited extent and consistency may involve theoretical and methodological unclarity (e.g., Zhang, 2018), but also a general lack of embeddedness in the empirical analytical tradition of media research (Verhoeven, 2009). A lion's share of the literature on reputation, including much of the work in which reputation is related to media coverage, is still entrenched in the functionalistic organization-centric research tradition (i.e., the dominant paradigm in public relations research and management studies) and is often lacking in terms of rigid empirical research. In addition, media scholars have, so far, not demonstrated too much interest in this domain of research either.

This section contends that the concept of *negativity* offers theoretical ground to connect extant agenda-setting literature on corporate reputation with empirical news research – especially economic news research. Most agenda-setting studies in the corporate domain have accounted for tone and several studies explicitly highlight the overrepresentation of negativity in corporate coverage – just as what is known of economic news more generally (see Sections 2 and 3) – and effects of negative news on corporate reputation (e.g., Jonkman, Trilling,

Verhoeven & Vliegenthart, 2020; Vogler & Eisenegger, 2020; Zhang, 2018). In addition, tone-effects may be contingent upon several conditions, for example, prior attitudes toward a corporate actor (e.g., Carroll & McComb, 2003; Einwiller, Carroll & Korn, 2010). Yet, the theoretical underpinning of these effects is limited and not sufficiently related to empirical research regarding news media and agenda setting.

In the remainder of this section, we outline literature on the relationship between negative news and reputation, and theoretically underpin three research expectations. In a following step, we present our research methods. We use data from the three-wave panel survey (held in 2015) in which the corporate reputation of twelve large Dutch firms is measured among members of the Dutch public (N = 3,270). We link these data to an automated content analyses of tone in online and printed newspaper coverage (N = 5,235) of four major Dutch outlets. Subsequently, we convey the results, and – in the last part of the section – draw conclusions, discuss results, and share implications for future research.

6.3 Negativity and Tone Effects

Scholars examining effects of tone on reputation have focused on the affective dimension of second-level agenda setting. While the cognitive dimension pertains to the salience of objects (e.g., a firm) or object-attributes (e.g., issues related to the firm), the affective dimension is concerned with the salience of evaluations (Carroll & McCombs, 2003). In the context of corporate news coverage, these evaluations (e.g., the tone with which an object or an attribute is described) are often studied at the overall level of the object (i.e., the firm) and/or attributes of the firm. Kiousis et al. (2007), for example, studied the relationship between tone salience in news coverage on the overall level of firm coverage and news on six different characteristics of a corporation (social responsibility, vision and leadership, products and services, emotional appeal, workplace environment, and financial performance). In this section, we focus specifically on the *overall* level of the firm.

Previous research in this context has not presented unequivocal conclusions. For example, Kiousis et al. (2007) did not find a relationship between tone and reputation. Drawing on the notions of the "bandwagon effect" and the "underdog effect," Meijer & Kleinnijenhuis (2006b) investigated tone effects on reputation for both "support and criticism news" and "success and failure news." Their study showed that both positive (bandwagon) and negative (underdog) news may lead to more favorable reputations. More recent work points in a different direction. A study by Zhang (2016) found positive significant correlations between media reputation (i.e., the general evaluation of a company in news coverage), and corporate reputation. In a subsequent study, comparing different favorability indexes, Zhang (2018) again found positive reputational effects of positive coverage and negative effects of negative coverage. Lastly, in a study on corporate CSR-news, Vogler & Eisenegger (2020) found a positive effect for tone on corporate reputation.

This last finding (just as the studies of Zhang, 2016, 2018) is line with the well-established idea in the political communication and economic news literature that affective attributes of news coverage are central determinants for attitudinal effects (Sheafer, 2007). Going beyond this, studies in corporate communication have recently started to observe that the impact negative news has on attitudes outweighs the effect of positive news (e.g., Vogler & Eisenegger, 2020; Zhang, 2018) – something many scholars in other domains of media-effect research have long shown (e.g., Kahneman & Tversky, 1982; Richey et al., 1975). As Section 4 in this Element demonstrates, this applies to economic news as well (see also, e.g., Damstra & Boukes, 2021; Hester & Gibson, 2003; Soroka, 2006). A common explanation for this – that humans have evolved in such a way that negative information has become more valuable than positive information – means tone weighs asymmetrically on people's attitudes (e.g., attitudes toward objects in the news; Baumeister et al., 2001). A second explanation is that we generally tend to expect marginally more positive information than negative information, so a violation of that assumption may produce asymmetrical responses to tone (Soroka, 2014).

In addition, conditional factors may affect the influence of negative news on corporate reputation. The notion of a "buffering effect" pertains to idea that the reputational consequences of negative information can be contingent upon other (individual) factors (Coombs & Holladay, 2006; Sohn & Lariscy, 2015). An experimental study on crisis communication by Sohn and Lariscy (2015) shows that a positive prior reputation can backfire when a firm's moral stance or conduct is challenged, but that it generally serves as a buffer for negative information. In a similar vein, Coombs and Holladay (2006) find support for a "halo effect"; the idea that positive prior reputation can function as shield for reputational damage. These findings follow the logic of a confirmation bias induced by cognitive dissonance: "reduction of dissonance is accomplished by selectively paying attention to information that is consistent with previously held beliefs ... weighing unequal values on different pieces of information" (Sohn & Lariscy, 2015, p. 239). This general logic has been robustly corroborated in the political communication literature (e.g., Arceneaux, Johnson & Cryderman, 2013; Levendusky, 2013; Stroud, 2010; Taber & Lodge, 2006).

For example, people are likely to interpret political news coverage in ways that match with their existing beliefs (Geiß & Schäfer, 2017).

Based on this, we expect that positive coverage of the company will improve the reputation of a company, while negative coverage will have the opposite effect. Additionally, one would anticipate the effects of negative coverage to be larger than those of positive coverage. And finally, the size of negative effects depends on the initial reputational attitude of an individual: the more positive the initial attitude, the weaker the negative effect of negative news on reputation.

6.4 Approach

We linked data from the earlier-mentioned three-wave panel survey among members of the Dutch public ($N = 3,270$) to an automated content analysis of company news in online and print news from four Dutch daily national news-papers *de Volkskrant, NRC Handelsblad, Telegraaf*, and *Metro* (print only) published in the first half of 2015. News content ($N = 5,235$) on the following twelve large Dutch corporations was analyzed for the periods between Wave 1 and Wave 2 and between Wave 2 and Wave 3 of the survey: ING (bank), Rabobank (bank), ABN AMRO (bank), SNS (bank), KLM Air France (airline), Heineken (brewer), Royal Dutch Shell (energy company), KPN (telecommunications); Philips (electronics and technology manufacturer), NS (Dutch national railway), PostNL (postal services), and V&D (department stores).

The SentiStrength algorithm (Thelwall, Buckley & Paltoglou, 2013; Thelwall et al., 2010) was used to measure positivity and negativity in each news article (see Jonkman, Boukes, Vliegenthart & Verhoeven, 2020 for a similar approach).

Table 5 The effect of media coverage on parliamentary questions in changing economic contexts

	Severe crisis	**No severe crisis**
Parliamentary questions (t-1)	0.467*** (0.053)	0.409*** (0.053)
Newspaper articles (t-1)	0.193*** (0.055)	0.387*** (0.052)
Change in unemployment (t-1)	0.442 (0.275)	0.504 (0.472)
Newspaper* Δ unemployment (t-1)	0.348* (0.152)	0.190 (0.436)
Constant	−0.008 (0.059)	−0.008 (0.061)
R^2 (N)	0.519 (266)	0.543 (284)

Note. Parliamentary questions and newspaper coverage have been standardized; fixed effects for countries are included (but not displayed). *p < 0.05; ** p < 0.01; *** p < 0.001

In addition to others who also validated the SentiStrength algorithm (e.g., Kroon & Van der Meer, 2018), we checked our assessment against a hand-coded subsample of the coverage of company news. Results of this validation check showed that the manual measures of negative and positive news correspond with our automated measure in a satisfactory way.

To be able to deduce to which content respondents were exposed during the period of study, we asked respondents in the first survey wave how frequently they used the examined media outlets on a scale of 0 (never) to 7 (seven days per week). In addition, we repeatedly measured corporate reputation for every company on a scale from 0 (very negative) to 10 (very positive) in all three survey waves (see, e.g., Meijer & Kleinnijenhuis, 2006a), allowing us to control for the respondents' existing reputational attitudes and establishing a solid causal link between the news to which they were exposed and their ensuing evaluations of an organization.

Linking the content analysis data to the panel survey data, we multiplied for each wave and for each individual the number of days (per week) a respondent reported being exposed to a newspaper or website by the tone scores of articles published in the particular outlet mentioning a particular corporation (linkage approach; see, e.g., De Vreese et al., 2017). Summing the exposure scores, finally, gave us, for each wave, an individual-level measure indicating the aggregated tone exposure scores for a certain firm for every individual respondent (see for a similar approach, e.g., Gattermann & De Vreese, 2017; Svensson et al., 2017).

Our observations are clustered within organizations and respondents, and time. In other words, each observation concerns individual x attitude toward company y at time t. Elsewhere, we used a cross-classified multilevel model to analyzse these data (see Jonkman, Boukes, Vliegenthart & Verhoeven, 2020). In this section, however, we opt for a more simplified and accessible model and rely on OLS regression models with a lagged dependent variable. Yet, the results demonstrated in the following are to a large extent comparable to those from more advanced models.

6.5 Results

Table 6 shows the aggregated tone scores of the panel survey data linked with the content analysis. The table reveals that the tone of company coverage in our media data is negative across the board, indicating that respondents in the panel survey sample have mainly been exposed to negative news, although with substantial cross-company and over-time variation: News coverage was particularly negative about ING (bank), ABN Amro (bank; especially before Wave 2), the railroad company NS, and Royal Dutch Airlines (KLM).

Table 6 Tone in news coverage

Variable	M Tone (W1-W2)	SD Tone (W1-W2)	M Tone (W2-W3)	SD Tone (W2-W3)
Shell	−7.67	(9.39)	−7.49	(9.36)
ING	−14.98	(18.51)	−12.52	(16.55)
Rabobank	−8.44	(1.65)	−8.63	(1.91)
Philips	−8.94	(11.31)	−6.21	(8.90)
Heineken	−3.56	(4.13)	−2.25	(3.28)
ABN Amro	−23.41	(28.93)	−1.83	(12.95)
KPN	−7.37	(9.22)	−5.98	(7.63)
PostNL	−3.02	(4.17)	−2.73	(3.57)
NS	−24.00	(32.27)	−24.05	(3.41)
SNS	−3.23	(3.98)	−0.65	(1.10)
V&D	−7.92	(9.47)	−3.16	(4.79)
KLM	−13.16	(16.78)	−11.54	(14.58)

Turning to analyses on the effects of tone and negativity on corporate reputation, Table 7 (Model 1) shows effects of tone to be in line with what we expected: Both positive and negative tone significantly influence reputation in the expected direction. We should, however, remark that the effect sizes are small. For example, for negative news, the *unstandardized* effect (not reported in table) is $b = -0.00078$ ($p < 0.001$). This implies that, on average, exposure to one extra news item about a corporation leads to a reputational decline of 0.00078 points (reputation measured on a scale of 0 to 10). This indicates that the impact of a single news article might be fairly limited. Yet, with aggregated exposure to negative news – which is more likely under circumstances of a structural negativity bias (see, e.g., Jonkman, Boukes, Vliegenthart & Verhoeven, 2020) – effects can be substantial.

Table 7 (Model 1) also indicates, in line with our expectations, that the standardized effect of negative news on reputation outweighs the standardized effect of positive news by more than twice ($-0.072/0.030 = -2.4$). An additional Wald test designates that the effect of negative news is indeed significantly stronger, $\chi^2 (1) = 73.55$, $p < 0.001$.

Finally, Table 7 (Model 2) shows a significant interaction effect between negative news and preexisting reputation ($b = 0.005$, $SE = 0.003$, $p < 0.05$), indicating the presence of a "buffering effect." The standardized effect of negative news on reputation in Model 2 is significant (-0.072, $p < 0.001$)

Table 7 The effect of tone and negative news on corporate reputation

	Model 1	**Model 2**
Lag reputation	0.645*** (0.005)	0.644*** (0.003)
Positive news	0.030*** (0.007)	0.030*** (0.005)
Negative news	−0.072*** (0.006)	−0.072*** (0.005)
Negative news x lag reputation		0.006** (0.003)
Constant	0.000 (0.005)	0.000 (0.005)
R^2 (N)	0.42 (78,480)	0.42 (78,480)

Note. Variables have been standardized. ** $p < 0.01$; *** $p < 0.001$

when preexisting reputation is 0. Yet, for each extra point on reputation, it changes by 0.006 ($p < 0.05$). This means that a positive prior reputation decreases the negative impact of negative tone in corporate news. This finding is in line with our expectations.

6.6 Conclusion

In line with findings from recent agenda-setting research in corporate communication, this section shows that affective attributes of news coverage on economic businesses can influence the evaluation of those businesses. More specifically, our data indicate that both positive and negative company news can influence corporate reputation in the expected direction (see, e.g., Vogler & Eisenegger, 2020; Zhang, 2018), but that negative news outweighs positive news in terms of impact (see, e.g., Vogler & Eisenegger, 2020; Zhang, 2018). Moreover, a positive prior reputational attitude toward a firm can serve as buffer for the impact of exposure to negative news (see, e.g., Coombs & Holladay, 2006; Sohn and Lariscy, 2015). Furthermore, our content analysis data reveals the dominance of negative news, which is in line both with the negativity bias discussed in previous sections and with recent findings in corporate news research (e.g., Jonkman, Boukes, Vliegenthart & Verhoeven, 2020; Vogler & Eisenegger, 2020; Zhang, 2018).

This section not only adds to our understanding of media effects in corporate communication, it also explicitly connects corporate news research with economic news research. In our theoretical framework, we showed that expectations regarding the reputational impact of negative news can be underpinned with theory developed in the realm of economic news. In addition, our findings on the influence of news on reputational attitudes (i.e., effects of positive and negative news; the asymmetrical impact of negative information) are in line with findings on the impact of economic news on economic attitudes (see discussion in sections 1 and 4). It demonstrates the generalizability of the media effects found in the previous sections beyond pure economic attitudes and evaluations and that these also apply to the financial/corporate context.

7 Learning about Economy through New Forms of Media

7.1 Introduction

In the previous sections, we have already demonstrated the pivotal role that media coverage on economic topics has on public opinion, parliamentary questions and debates, and corporate reputation. Indeed, as reflected in this Element, the research on the interdependence of economic developments, media, politics and public opinion has been dominated by a focus on the traditional journalistic media. In related fields, such as political communication (Holbert, 2013; Shehata & Strömbäck, 2018) and science communication (Cacciatore et al., 2020; Hwong et al., 2017), however, attention has gradually shifted to also include newer forms of media including social network sites and infotainment formats. This has so far rarely been the case for economic news.

The relevance of incorporating these new media formats in the research on economic news effects is twofold. Theoretically, they provide citizens with a different kind of news message, which may accordingly have different kinds of effects. Practically, these alternative forms of news may reach a different audience that has partly tuned out from the regular news media. This section looks into the effects that the usage of social media – the two most popular social network sites in particular: *Facebook* and *Twitter* – and political satire have on the acquisition of knowledge about economic events.

7.2 Acquiring Knowledge about Economic Events

Whereas the previous sections have looked mostly at changes in the perceptions and attitudes of citizens, the current section embarks on an investigation of how people's *knowledge* about economic issues may be influenced by the consumption of social media and political satire. Regarding the economic topic in particular, very little is known about the impact these newer forms of news might have. It is important to first assess whether people learn anything from these media, before looking into their further effects. After all, knowledge is a crucial determinant of how people shape their political opinions (Lenz, 2009), but probably also has a strong impact on economic impressions, such as consumer confidence: To make a reasonable estimation of how the economy at large is performing, and eventually to reward or punish a government for that (Mutz, 1992; Sanders, 2000), people will first have to learn the basic facts.

Traditionally, people learn about such facts through journalistic news media (Jerit, Barabas & Bolsen, 2006; Shehata et al., 2015; Tichenor, Donohue & Olien, 1970), and we have found this with respect to economic news too (Boukes & Vliegenthart, 2019). However, with the fragmentation of the media landscape, this journalistic dominance will be weaker than two decades ago (Prior, 2007). Many people may prefer entertainment programming over news programs and the news audience, therefore, has shrunk considerably (Mindich, 2005). Moreover, an increasing number of people seem to intentionally avoid the news (Skovsgaard & Andersen, 2020), because they experience that following the news has a negative impact on their mental well-being (Boukes & Vliegenthart, 2017) or they have lost trust in the news media (Tsfati & Cappella, 2003). The question, then, is whether new forms of news may fill this gap: *Can social media and satire also educate citizens about the important economic events?*

Although people might not consume comedy programs or social media with the intention to learn about economic news, this does not exclude the possibility that they – inadvertently or not – acquire knowledge from these platforms. In the academic literature on soft news, this has been coined "piggybacking" (Baum, 2003, p. 30): Many citizens may not perceive (economic) news valuable enough to spend their time on watching or reading the news; however, when this information comes together with something they perceive as valuable or enjoyable, they may still learn about it (i.e., the trade-off of acquiring knowledge is low enough and ignoring the information would even be a bigger loss). To achieve learning effects, though, such media, of course, still have to present the relevant information.

7.3 Contents and Effects in Political Domain: Political Satire

Although some doubt the democratic contribution of satire shows (Hart & Hartelius, 2007), its producers are actually striving for traditional journalistic values, such as factuality, political relevance and monitoring the powerful (Koivukoski & Ödmark, 2020). Empirical content analyses of political satire indeed demonstrate the potential of this genre to inform the audience about politically substantive issues. A large majority of the humoristic content in a Swiss satire show revolves around current affairs and politics with more often a focus on the actual substance of the issue than on the involved political personalities (Matthes & Rauchfleisch, 2013). Similarly, late-night shows in the United States carry a majority of "informative" jokes that provide real information about actual news events (Brewer & Marquardt, 2007; Haigh & Heresco, 2010). A comparison with actual newscasts even showed that the amount of substantive information did not differ from satire programming (Fox, Koloen & Sahin, 2007). Accordingly, satire might create an effective counter-narrative, also for complicated economic issues (Nitsch & Lichtenstein, 2019), and encourage a broader public understanding (Bessant, 2017).

Given these content features of political satire, it is not surprising that the genre is able to cause actual knowledge gains among its audience (Becker, 2013). Whereas previous research suggested that knowledge could especially be transferred for "easy" topics (i.e., facts that most people already know), this finding has been challenged in more recent years. With the satire genre developing into a format that more closely reflects in-depth journalistic styles of coverage – for instance, *Last Week Tonight* in the United States or *Zondag met Lubach* in the Netherlands (Nieuwenhuis, 2018) – one can conclude that satire may also increase knowledge of more complicated topics. Concretely, satire exposure has been positively correlated with knowledge about net neutrality (Becker & Bode, 2018) and campaign financing (Hardy et al., 2014). Accordingly, we investigate how political satire consumption influences the knowledge about economic affairs.

7.4 Contents and Effects in Political Domain: Social Network Sites

Previous studies found mixed results regarding the potential of social media to inform citizens about public affairs. Whereas some studies find negative effects or null findings (Dimitrova et al., 2014; Lee & Xenos, 2019), others find positive outcomes when people use social media for information purposes (Feezell, 2018; Yoo & Gil de Zúñiga, 2014). The reason for the contradictory conclusions is probably two-fold: First, studies that found positive effect often had measurements of social media use that included the actual intention to learn something about the news; second, many existing studies conflate social media platforms, whereas they have very different content features.

This section, therefore, investigates the effects of *Facebook* and *Twitter* separately and analyzes the effect of general platform consumption (i.e., how frequently do people use these networks time-wise). The two platforms differ on various aspects. Most crucially, *Facebook* is built on the idea of two-way relationships in relatively closed circuits (Ju, Jeong & Chyi, 2014; Lee & Oh, 2013) and does not permit account anonymity; in contrast, most user-pairs on *Twitter* are uni-directional with one user following another, but not vice-versa (Davenport et al., 2014). This platform infrastructure is also reflected by the actual motivations of citizens for using them: *Facebook* is mainly used for social purposes and entertainment (Hughes et al., 2012). Accordingly, its algorithm decides that people see only a few news stories in their *Facebook* timelines (Wang, 2017), while personal messages of friends and family are prioritized. The opposite is true for *Twitter*: People use it for information purposes (Costera Meijer & Groot Kormelink, 2015) and the trending topics as well as popular retweets reflect the news headlines (Kwak et al., 2010). Finally, *Twitter*'s short message format has been shown to ease learning (Gleason, 2013). In other words, for economic news, users might be more dependent on Twitter than on Facebook for information. Accordingly, it is unlikely that the effects of both social network sites are uniform. Therefore, we ask the question how consumption of Facebook and Twitter influences knowledge about economic affairs?

Barabas et al. (2014) classified knowledge on two dimensions: a topic dimension (general vs. policy-specific) and a temporal dimension (static vs. surveillance). We investigate policy-specific surveillance knowledge from the political-economic domain, because such dynamic facts (e.g., unemployment rates, recent news events) are the type of knowledge most likely to be learned from the media. After all, static types of knowledge (e.g., the number of seats in Parliament or what "inflation" would mean) is most likely the outcome of education and long-term learning processes. To investigate how media influence citizens' knowledge, it thus makes sense to focus on how knowledge of recent facts differs across users of certain media outlets. After all, it is unlikely that these facts are learned somewhere else (i.e., facts were not known when most respondents were still in school), thus, excluding alternative or confounding explanations.

7.5 Approach

The research questions of this section were analyzed with data of the three-wave panel survey that was also employed in Section 6. The panel survey was conducted by *I&O Research* in the first half year of 2015 with an eight-week interval. 6,386 respondents completed the first survey wave, and 3,270 of them all waves.

The first survey contained detailed media exposure measurements. Following the recommendation of Andersen et al. (2016), we asked respondents to report the specific frequency (i.e., number of days per week or month) with which they consumed specific outlets. This question was asked for the specific social network sites (*Facebook* and *Twitter*) and the most popular Dutch satire show, *Zondag Met Lubach* (*ZML*). Dummy variables were created to distinguish *Facebook*-users (49.6 percent of sample), *Twitter*-users (13.3 percent), and *ZML*-viewers (11.6 percent) from nonusers and nonviewers.

The dataset allowed us to test three different subtypes of policy-specific surveillance knowledge: knowledge about current affairs news events, specific policy, and statistical economic indicators. Regarding the latter, respondents were asked to estimate the exact percentage of people in the Netherlands who were unemployed (similar as in the study reported in Section 4). By subtracting the actual percentage from the estimate (i.e., 7 percent), a variable could be calculated that measured exact knowledge of this important statistical indicator. Unemployment estimates above 40 percent were excluded as outliers (4 percent of the data): 17 percent of respondents knew the answer exactly, and the average deviation from the actual unemployment rate was 5.91 percent ($SD = 8.25$)

Regarding the second measurement of knowledge – knowing the correct answer to a question about a specific policy – we verify Druckman (2005): "Learning information from a given medium requires that the medium includes that information" (p. 466). Concretely, we asked a multiple-choice question about the meaning of TTIP, which is the *Transatlantic Trade and Investment Partnership* between the European Union and the United States. This topic was the main focus of one *Zondag met Lubach* (*ZML*, satire show) episode on March 15, 2015, which happened to be exactly between the first and second wave of the panel survey. The question, accordingly, was asked in the second wave. The satire episode also sparked quite some (social) media attention, hence, social media consumption may also increase the probability of a correct answer. A total of 60 percent of the respondents answered the question correctly.

Finally, every survey wave included several multiple-choice knowledge questions about political-economic events that had just been in the news. Inspired by Kalogeropoulos, Albæk et al. (2015), the first survey wave had five such questions (about the current interest rate; the name of the Finance minister; name of the Managing Director of the IMF; most important Dutch trading partners; and credit rating of the Netherlands). The summed index of the number of correct answers functioned as a control variable in all the analyses: It measures people's general knowledge level. The likelihood of finding any effects of media consumption on top of this that are caused by a confounding variable, therefore, is very low.

In Wave 2 and Wave 3, four additional questions were asked to tap how much knowledge people gained between the waves. These questions concerned topics unknown before the previous wave (i.e., they had not taken place yet) and were, thus, most likely learned through media consumption. Specifically, questions were asked about which government-owned bank came into disrepute because of the bonuses of its directors (i.e., *ABN Amro*), a law that was approved by Parliament with a direct impact on

Dutch employees (i.e., allowing flexible working times), the semipublic corporation Timo Huges worked for before he resigned after problems with public procurements (i.e., *NS*, Dutch Railway), and the percentage of economic growth as predicted by the Dutch National Bank (i.e., 2 percent). Additional analyses of regular news media confirmed that these all were frequently covered in the lead-up to the respective survey wave. On average, people answered 2.88 questions correctly (*SD* = 1.00).

Analyses controlled for the consumption of regular news media and interpersonal communication about political and economic topics to make sure that effects were the outcome of the newer forms of media (satire and social network sites) and not alternative sources of information. Analysis also controlled for age, gender, education and political interest.

7.6 Results

Table 8 shows a series of regression models predicting the uptake of knowledge about economic affairs. Some consistent patterns were found for the control variables. Overall, more knowledge was gained by the following types of people: older respondents, men, people with higher levels of education, and those with more political interest and who talked more frequently about economic and political affairs. These findings are in line with existing research of political knowledge effects, which strengthens confidence in the measurement validity of our dependent variables.

Mixed findings were yielded for the effects of traditional news media outlets. Remarkably, no significant effects ($p < 0.05$) were yielded for the consumption of print newspapers. More frequently visiting news websites, however, consistently increased the probability of (more) correct knowledge answers. And for television, the findings were likewise mixed: Whereas more television news consumption increased knowledge about current affairs events, it decreased the likelihood of knowing what TTIP was and worsened the estimate of the unemployment rate.

Model 1 in Table 8 shows the effects on respondents' estimate of the unemployment rate in the Netherlands at the moment of the first survey. Higher scores on the dependent variable mean that people's estimation is less accurate (i.e., bigger difference compared to the actual unemployment rate of 7 percent). The results, first, show that the effects of the satire show and *Twitter* were insignificant. However, *Facebook* consumption had a positive effect. It shows that *Facebook* users, on average, were about 0.87 points (rounded: 1 percent) less accurate than non-*Facebook* users. Thus, *Facebook* consumption has made the estimate of the unemployment rate *worse*. This finding is not

Table 8 Regression models predicting the acquisition of policy-specific surveillance knowledge about economic topics

	Model 1: Δ estimate unemployment rate				Model 2: Policy knowledge: TTIP				Model 3: Knowledge about current affairs events			
	B	(SE)	b*	p	b	(SE)	OR	p	b	(SE)	z	p
Intercept	16.11	(0.75)		0.000	−2.95	(0.27)	0.05	0.000	0.43	(0.05)	8.85	0.000
Existing knowledge	−1.55	(0.10)	−0.21	0.000	0.49	(0.04)	1.63	0.000	0.09	(0.01)	14.30	0.000
Age	−0.03	(0.01)	−0.04	0.002	0.01	(0.00)	1.01	0.111	0.00	(0.00)	2.88	0.004
Female	0.04	(0.23)	0.18	0.000	−0.37	(0.08)	0.69	0.000	−0.08	(0.01)	−6.23	0.000
Education	−0.77	(0.07)	−0.14	0.000	0.21	(0.02)	1.23	0.000	0.01	(0.00)	3.65	0.000
Political interest	−0.34	(0.06)	−0.08	0.000	0.12	(0.02)	1.13	0.000	0.02	(0.00)	5.38	0.000
Interpersonal talk	−0.16	(0.04)	−0.06	0.000	0.06	(0.01)	1.06	0.000	0.01	(0.00)	2.81	0.005
TV news consumption	0.09	(0.02)	0.05	0.000	−0.02	(0.01)	0.98	0.010	0.00	(0.00)	3.60	0.000
Newspaper consumption	−0.03	(0.02)	−0.02	0.179	0.00	(0.01)	1.00	0.631	0.00	(0.00)	1.56	0.119
News website consumption	−0.02	(0.01)	−0.02	0.072	0.03	(0.01)	1.03	0.000	0.00	(0.00)	3.85	0.000
Satire: ZML	−0.40	(0.27)	−0.02	0.131	0.64	(0.12)	1.90	0.000	0.00	(0.02)	0.04	0.966
SNS: Facebook	0.87	(0.20)	0.05	0.000	−0.19	(0.07)	0.82	0.009	−0.04	(0.01)	−3.07	0.002
SNS: Twitter	−0.17	(0.28)	−0.01	0.546	0.32	(0.12)	1.37	0.007	0.05	(0.02)	2.75	0.006
N	6,059				4,264				3,240			
R^2	0.20				0.16	(Pseudo)			0.02	(Pseudo)		

Note. Model 1 applied OLS regression, Model 2 logistic regression and Model 3 Poisson regression. Cells contain unstandardized (b) coefficients with robust clustered standard errors (SE) in parentheses, and probabilities (p; two-tailed). Additionally, Model 1 presents standardized effect coefficients (b*), Model 2 odds rations (OR), and Model 3 z-values to give an indication of effect strength.

unique. Cacciatore et al. (2018) also found that political knowledge scores were negatively associated with *Facebook* use. Moreover, Model 2 and Model 3 also report negative effects of *Facebook* use. The odds of knowing what TTIP stands for was 0.82 times lower for *Facebook* users (Model 2), and on average they answered 0.04 fewer questions correctly.

Model 2 shows the effects on knowledge of the TTIP trade agreement. As mentioned previously, *Facebook* had a negative effect; however, the likelihood of knowing what TTIP meant was higher among the satire consumers and the *Twitter* users. A strong effect was yielded for *ZML* consumption. Viewers of this program were about two times (OR = 1.90) more likely to know the answer to this question than non-viewers. The reason is obvious: This show dedicated a whole episode to the topic and viewers were likely to remember this. A positive effect was also found of *Twitter* use on knowledge of TTIP. The odds of knowing the correct answer was 1.37 times higher for users of *Twitter* compared to non-users. One likely explanation is that *Zondag met Lubach* viewers tweeted about this topic and, thereby, informed the non-*ZML* viewers who are users of this social network.

Finally, Model 3 shows the effects on the composite knowledge index about current affairs events. The satire viewers did not differ from the non-satire viewers ($p = 0.966$), which is probably because the topics in the multiple-choice questions were not discussed in the satire show. Whereas a negative effect was found for *Facebook*, *Twitter* users knew more answers than non-*Twitter* users. On average, they answered 0.05 more questions correctly. Thus, *Twitter* has the ability to educate people about economic news events.

7.7 Conclusion

All in all, this section presents mixed evidence for the idea that new forms of media – satire and social network sites – educate citizens about economic news in times when people increasingly avoid the mainstream news media (Skovsgaard & Andersen, 2020). Satire will only increase knowledge about a specific topic if it pays extensive attention to it: satire shows only present a small number of topics while regular newscasts presents multitude facts in a broadcast. This is in line with previous experimental findings by Young and Hoffman (2012) demonstrating that satire contributes to current affairs knowledge, but not to, for example, civics knowledge. Hence, satire can encourage economic knowledge acquisition, but only on a limited number of subjects. The learning effects of *Twitter* are more *all-round*, in the sense that its use also positively affected uptake of economic knowledge about current affairs events. This is not surprising, because the most popular posts on *Twitter* are an accurate reflection of the news headlines (Kwak et al., 2010). Nevertheless, *Twitter* use did not improve the accuracy of unemployment rate estimates. The information about this sensitive issue is, possibly, overshadowed by the diversity of voices and personal interpretations regarding this topic: Soroka et al. (2018), for example, found a clear positivity bias on *Twitter* regarding posts about unemployment, which might skew people's perceptions about this statistic. Additionally, as Section 4 also demonstrated, this type of economic knowledge is not straightforwardly affected by media exposure and a range of other factors might account for the accuracy of this type of perception.

Whereas satire and *Twitter* positively influenced certain dimensions of economic knowledge, the opposite was found for *Facebook*: The use of this social network site had an unambiguous negative effect on all three the types of economic surveillance knowledge. This platform – at least in the context of the Netherlands and regarding the topic economic– thus seems to be pure entertainment without any alleviating potential. Although it is tempting to fall into a negative narrative similar to Postman's (1986) work, *Amusing Ourselves to Death*, about the rise of television, this would ignore some positive effects that have also been found; for example, regarding engagement with the news (Oeldorf-Hirsch, 2018) or strengthening citizens' feeling that they understand the news (Müller, Schneiders & Schäfer, 2016). Additional analysis of our data, however, show that the negative effects of *Facebook* usage on the accuracy of unemployment rate estimation and knowledge about current affairs events were especially strong for those already having a lower level of existing knowledge (see also Boukes, 2019b): it is especially the already uninformed citizens who are misinformed or distracted from knowledge acquisition; thus, amplifying the knowledge gap in society.

Twitter and, to a lesser degree, satire consumption positively influenced knowledge acquisition about economic topics. Whether or not this knowledge gain is deliberate or a positive side effect when media are used to satisfy other needs or gratifications, dependence on them is fruitful. Research has shown that these knowledge effects, eventually, may carry even further. Acquiring knowledge is the first step that might set in motion a range of other cognitive and attitudinal processes. For example, it might better inform people about the economic issue positions of political parties and thereby increase the "quality" of their votes (Lenz, 2009). Moreover, it might spark agenda-setting processes that eventually can cause regular media to report on it and encourage political elites to discuss the issue (Boukes, 2019a; McCombs & Shaw, 1972). The conclusion of this section, however, is that new forms of media might indeed contribute to the knowledge of economic affairs, but that it is only specific platforms (*Twitter* and satire; i.e., not *Facebook*) that encourage knowledge acquisition on specific dimensions of economic knowledge (i.e., estimates of unemployment statistics were unaffected). Hence, one should be careful not to draw too strong and general – negative or positive – conclusions.

8 Conclusion
8.1 How Do Media Cover the economy?

This Element has set out to answer two important questions relating to economic news: that pertaining to news production (antecedents) and to the effects this news may have. Building upon a range of rich datasets, we have identified important mechanisms that can account for both the content and consequences of economic news. Thereby, we expanded existing theoretical frameworks to the domain of economic news.

We identified two clear features of economic coverage that are present, irrespective of outlet, content or context. The first is a persistent negativity bias, established in Section 2 a cross-national comparison of economic news coverage by international press agencies. The interview study in Section 3 disentangles the underlying mechanisms, confirming on the one hand the inherent higher newsworthiness of negative news, but also the differential nature of negative developments that often occur unexpectedly and evolve rapidly, amplifying their newsworthiness even further. Second, limited frame variation and a lack of critical perspectives is widely present. This finding confirms existing research on mass media coverage providing more space to authoritative actors and being reluctant to prominently include those that challenge the status quo. An additional explanation is provided by the interviews with journalists in Section 3: The economy is a highly complex issue and journalists, as well as news consumers, often lack the capacity to grasp the economy in all its facets, again strengthening the tendency to bring coverage in established terminology and frames of reference, and often simplifying the complex matters.

8.2 What Are the Effects of Economic News Coverage?
8.2.1 Another Negativity Bias

In mapping the consequences of economic news, we firstly focused on people's economic attitudes and perceptions. Sections 4 and 6 discuss a second negativity bias: negative media coverage is found to provoke stronger effects on people's attitudes and perceptions than positive coverage. This impact is strongest for sociotropic and egotropic economic perceptions, but has more far-reaching (indirect) consequences as well. Economic evaluations have an impact on the evaluations of the incumbent government and electoral preferences. Section 6 confirms the asymmetric impact of negative versus positive information in the context of the reputation of companies. Reputation, like consumer confidence, might take a long time to acquire, but is easy to lose. Also politicians are in similar ways affected by negative coverage as regular citizens (Section 5), with increasing levels of negative media content yielding more parliamentary questions about economic problems. Both reputation and parliamentary behavior are context dependent: Good reputations serve as a buffer against the detrimental effects of negative coverage, and effects of negative coverage on the parliamentary agenda are less strong in national contexts that suffer (comparatively) from a deep economic crisis. The latter finding is in line with the idea of media dependency: when abundant signals about the (bad) situation are present, media add little to the information politicians receive and they will respond less.

8.2.2 Contingency of Framing and Knowledge Effects

Much of our assessments of media effects rely on the tone of coverage. The empirical analyses in Section 4 use tone as a key aspect of economic information that is presented to participants, but, maybe surprisingly, it has little impact when the outcome variable asks for an assessment of the actual level of unemployment; possibly, this is due to the specifics of this topic and the related complex phrasing, with declining unemployment trends actually being positive news, and increasing unemployment implying negative developments.

Another key aspect of coverage is the attribution of responsibility and blame. Who can be held accountable for an economic problem is, as we saw in Section 2, a defining element of the frames that can be identified during the economic crisis. While the Dutch case demonstrates only limited attribution of responsibility to the government – much in line with the lack of alternative critical framing toward those in power – we do find that if media attribute blame to the government, evaluations of government's performance decrease, as do the popularity and electoral fortunes of the incumbent political parties. Remarkably enough, but in line with negativity bias and what we found when it comes to reputation of companies, positive evaluations of the government in news coverage (i.e., being credited for economic performances) do not increase its popularity (Damstra, Bourkes & Vliegenthart, 2021).

A final and important insight related to the effects of economic news coverage is that they are not constrained to the mainstream outlets. Section 7 examined to what extent people learn from information presented on social media and through satire. The analyses demonstrate that they do, but not equally for all platforms and all types of knowledge. Most notably, and in line with the gratification many users seek in each medium, Facebook stands out in *not* contributing to knowledge (about the economy), while Twitter and satire programs do. As these alternative information sources inform citizens about the economy, they may be equally likely to also affect their economic attitudes.

What is clear from looking into media effects is that they cannot only be attributed to specific content characteristics and can differ for different outcome variables; they are additionally largely contingent on individual (e.g., initial knowledge and reputation assessments), channel (e.g., different social media), context (severity of the crisis) and issue (level of specificity) characteristics. Many of those characteristics relate to the degree of media dependence and the extent to which media contain (additional) information that is not available through other channels or through direct experience. What the analyses jointly show is that media effects differ, often in logical ways, but also that differences can stem from a wide range of factors.

8.3 Implications

Our empirical findings can have far-reaching implications. The impact of economic news on people's economic opinions and perceptions may have subsequent effects on economic behavior. Thinking again of the everyday citizens who rely for their economic perceptions partly on the news encountered through reading the newspaper, scrolling on a phone and watching the evening news, previous work has demonstrated how economic evaluations affect consumption expenditure (Ludvigson, 2004; Nguyen & Claus, 2013). This behavior of individual consumers ultimately translates into economic fluctuations on the aggregate level as well (Matsusaka & Sbordone, 1995). In addition, work by Kleinnijenhuis et al. (2013) finds evidence for a direct effect of financial news on financial markets. These studies suggest that the relationship between economic news and economic reality may not be entirely unidirectional, as economic news may affect economic opinions that, in turn, may influence economic behavior and, ultimately, economic conditions. Given the negativity biases in coverage and effects, this might yield downward spirals with negative economic coverage resulting in worsening economic conditions that again attract (disproportionate) negative attention, etcetera.

Furthermore, as it is often not in the interest of financial institutions, corporations and other economic actors to be in the news, most of them will also not actively try to get access to the media agenda. Consequently, a very substantial part of economic reality goes uncovered and is not monitored at all. In a globalized economy in which extremely powerful economic actors operate worldwide, some with larger economies of scale than whole countries (Van Dalen et al., 2018), this lack of public and political control is problematic from a democratic point of view. It follows that the public is informed selectively and that they respond selectively as well. Media portray economic reality as being vastly less diverse than it in fact is. This implies that, to the public at large, certain dimensions or interpretations of economic reality simply remain out of sight and citizens are denied the opportunity to develop opinions about them.

The identified biases in economic news reporting and the effects of media coverage raise some normative questions about economic journalism. Does the mainstream press fall short in relation to their task and responsibilities in democratic society? The answer depends on the democratic model one deems desirable as this determines the news standards by which the quality of journalism can be evaluated. Adopting the idea that citizens should be able to make informed political judgments at the ballot box, the information provided to them by the news media should be proportional, in correspondence with reality, diverse in terms of views offered, and critical of power structures (Strömbäck, 2005: 338–339). Given the biases identified in Sections 2 and 3, one may conclude that mainstream economic news does not meet those criteria.

However, evaluations of journalism in democratic theory are often, in essence, a discussion of the normative functions we have in mind for *political* journalism (see, for example, Ferree et al., 2002; Strömbäck, 2005). Notwithstanding the strong connection between the economic realm and the world of politics, there are differences between the two that should not be set aside. Most importantly, the price of information differs. In politics, there is a mutual dependency between journalists and political actors. Journalists need their sources for inside information, but sources are also dependent on journalists to get their information out and reach the electorate. In economics, another dynamic applies, because it often is not in the interest of financial institutions, corporations and other powerful actors to be in the news; there is much less willingness to share data, making relevant information difficult to obtain (Dyck & Zingales, 2003). This restricted information availability combined with the high complexity of economic reality presents economic journalists with additional challenges that should be taken into account when evaluating their news products.

Given the economic power structures that arrange the world we live in, economic journalism is nevertheless of utmost importance. Precisely because of the challenges discussed here, economic journalists should be given additional resources to look at larger issues rather than being absorbed by the event-centered focus typical of the daily news cycle. This also implies that outlets should not prioritize generalist journalism over specialist journalism, as specialized knowledge is indispensable to critically assess complex content. Investing resources in mainstream economic journalism may require a major turnaround – as this is far from self-evident in current profit-driven media markets – but it would prove to be worth the investment. Journalism education could put more emphasis on economic and financial topics, or people with an educational background in economics or finance could be additionally trained to work on these topics as journalists.

Economic news comes with unique features rendering it a perfect test case for research on media biases and media effects. In contrast to other news areas such as crime, foreign affairs or the environment, there is considerable standardized economic data available. This allows researchers to make structural comparisons between economic reality, economic news and public perceptions, laying bare persistent biases in economic news reporting and public opinion. In addition, people's economic opinions are also closely monitored on individual and aggregate levels, which allows researchers to examine the effects of economic news in longitudinal and even cross-national designs. We expect that the biases and asymmetric news effects identified in this Element are not confined to economic news reporting. In fact, other news domains such as immigration or the environment may exhibit similar or even greater degrees of bias and subsequent (asymmetric) news effects. We hope that we have set a useful standard to further examine the tripartite relationship between social reality, news coverage, and public opinion, in the realm of economics and beyond.

References

Ahluwalia, R. (2002). How prevalent is the negativity effect in consumer environments? *Journal of Consumer Research, 29,* 270–279.

Andersen, K., de Vreese, C. H., & Albæk, E. (2016). Measuring media diet in a high-choice environment: Testing the list-frequency technique. *Communication Methods and Measures, 10,* 81–98.

Arceneaux, K., Johnson, M., & Cryderman, J. (2013). Communication, persuasion, and the conditioning value of selective exposure: Like minds may unite and divide but they mostly tune out. *Political communication, 30,* 213–231.

Ball-Rokeach, S. J. (1985). The origins of individual media-system dependency: A sociological framework. *Communication Research, 12,* 485–451.

Barabas, J., Jerit, J., Pollock, W., & Rainey, C. (2014). The question(s) of political knowledge. *American Political Science Review, 108,* 840–855.

Baum, M. A. (2003). *Soft news goes to war: Public opinion and american foreign policy in the new media age.* Princeton, NJ: Princeton University Press.

Baumeister, R. F., Bratslavsky, E., Finkenauer, C., & Vohs, K. D. (2001). Bad is stronger than good. *Review of General Psychology, 5,* 323–337.

Baumgartner, F. R., & Jones, B. D. (2010). *Agendas and instability in American politics.* Chicago: University of Chicago Press.

Becker, A. B. (2013). What about those interviews? The impact of exposure to political comedy and cable news on factual recall and anticipated political expression. *International Journal of Public Opinion Research, 25,* 344–356.

Becker, A. B., & Bode, L. (2018). Satire as a source for learning? The differential impact of news versus satire exposure on net neutrality knowledge gain. *Information, Communication & Society, 21,* 612–625.

Bennett, W. L. (1990). Toward a theory of press-state relations in the United States. *Journal of Communication, 40,* 103–127.

Berry, M. (2016). No alternative to austerity: how BBC broadcast news reported the deficit debate. *Media, Culture & Society,* 38, 844–863.

Bessant, J. (2017). New politics and satire: The euro financial crisis and the one-finger salute. *Information, Communication & Society, 20,* 1057–1072.

Blood, D. J., & Phillips, P. C. (1995). Recession headline news, consumer sentiment, the state of the economy and presidential popularity: A time series analysis 1989–1993. *International Journal of Public Opinion Research, 7,* 2–22.

Boomgaarden, H. G., Van Spanje, J., Vliegenthart, R., & De Vreese, C. H. (2011). Covering the crisis: Media coverage of the economic crisis and citizens' economic expectations. *Acta Politica, 46,* 353–379.

Boukes, M. (2019a). Agenda-setting with satire: How political satire increased TTIP's saliency on the public, media, and political agenda. *Political Communication, 36,* 426–451.

Boukes, M. (2019b). Social network sites and acquiring current affairs knowledge: The impact of twitter and facebook usage on learning about the news. *Journal of Information Technology & Politics, 16,* 36–51.

Boukes, M., van de Velde, B., Araujo, T., & Vliegenthart, R. (2020). What's the tone? Easy doesn't do it: Analyzing performance and agreement between off-the-shelf sentiment analysis tools. *Communication Methods and Measures, 14,* 83–104.

Boukes, M., & Vliegenthart, R. (2017). News consumption and its unpleasant side effect. *Journal of Media Psychology, 29,* 137–147.

Boukes, M., & Vliegenthart, R. (2019). The knowledge gap hypothesis across modality: Differential acquisition of knowledge from television news, newspapers, and news websites. *International Journal of Communication, 13,* 3650–3671.

Boukes, M., & Vliegenthart, R. (2020). A general pattern in the construction of economic newsworthiness? Analyzing news factors in popular, quality, regional, and financial newspapers. *Journalism, 21,* 279–230.

Boukes, M., Damstra, A., & Vliegenthart, R. (2019). Media effects across time and subject: How news coverage affects two out of four attributes of consumer confidence. Communication Research. Advance online publication, 1–23.

Boukes, M., Van Esch, F. A. W. J., Snellens, J., Steenman, S., & Vliegenthart, R. (forthcoming). Studying the relationship between news exposure and cognitive complexity with cognitive mapping. Public Opinion Quarterly.

Boydstun, A. E., Highton, B., & Linn, S. (2018). Assessing the relationship between economic news coverage and mass economic attitudes. *Political Research Quarterly, 71*(4), 989–100.

Boydstun, A. E., Ledgerwood, A., & Sparks, J. (2019). A negativity bias in reframing shapes political preferences even in partisan contexts. *Social Psychological and Personality Science, 10*(1), 53–61.

Brewer, P. R., & Marquardt, E. (2007). Mock news and democracy: Analyzing the daily show. *Atlanticournal of Communication, 15,* 249–267.

Cacciatore, M. A., Becker, A. B., Anderson, A. A., & Yeo, S. K. (2020). Laughing with science: The influence of audience approval on engagement. *Science Communication, 42,* 195–217.

Cacciatore, M. A., Yeo, S. K., Scheufele, D. A., Xenos, M. A., Brossard, D., & Corley, E. A. (2018). Is Facebook making us dumber? Exploring social media use as a predictor of political knowledge. *Journalism & Mass Communication Quarterly*, *95*, 404–424.

Carroll G. E., & McCombs M. (2003). Agenda-setting effects of business news on the public's images and on opinions about major corporations. *Corporate Reputation Review*, *6*, 36–46.

Cobb, R. W., & Elder, C. D. (1971). The politics of agenda-building: An alternative perspective for modern democratic theory. *Journal of Politics*, *33*, 892–915.

Coombs, W., & Holladay, S. J. (2006). Unpacking the halo effect: Reputation and crisis management. *Journal of Communication Management*, *10*, 123–137.

Corbin, J., & Strauss, A. (2014). *Basics of qualitative research: Techniques and procedures for developing grounded theory*. London: Sage.

Costera Meijer, I., & Groot Kormelink, T. (2015). Checking, sharing, clicking and linking. *Digital Journalism*, *3*, 664–679.

Damstra, A. (2019). Disentangling Economic News Effects: The Impact of Tone, Uncertainty, and Issue on Public Opinion. *International Journal of Communication*, *13*, 5205–5224.

Damstra, A., & Boukes, M. (2021). The economy, the news, and the public: A longitudinal study of the impact of economic news on economic evaluations and expectations. *Communication Research*, 41, 26–50.

Damstra, A., & De Swert, K. (2020). The making of economic news: Dutch economic journalists contextualizing their work. *Journalism*. Advance online publication.

Damstra, A., & Vliegenthart, R. (2018). (Un)covering the economic crisis? *Journalism Studies*, *19*, 983–1003.

Damstra, A., Boukes, M., & Vliegenthart, R. (2021). Taking it personal or national? Understanding the indirect effects of economic news on government support. *West European Politics*, *44*, 253–274.

Davenport, S. W., Bergman, S. M., Bergman, J. Z., & Fearrington, M. E. (2014). Twitter versus Facebook: Exploring the role of narcissism in the motives and usage of different social media platforms. *Computers in Human Behavior*, 32, 212–220.

De Vreese, C. H., Boukes, M., Schuck, A., Vliegenthart, R., Bos, L., & Lelkes, Y. (2017). Linking survey and media content data: Opportunities, considerations, and pitfalls. *Communication Methods and Measures*, *11*, 221–244.

Deephouse, D. L. (2000). Media reputation as a strategic resource: An integration of mass communication and resource-based theories. *Journal of Management*, *26*, 1091–1112.

Dimitrova, D. V., Shehata, A., Strömbäck, J., & Nord, L. W. (2014). The effects of digital media on political knowledge and participation in election campaigns: Evidence from panel data. *Communication Research, 41*, 95–118.

Doms, M. E., & Morin, N. J. (2004). *Consumer sentiment, the economy, and the news media*. Washington, DC: Federal Reserve Board.

Doyle, G. (2006). Financial news journalism: A post-Enron analysis of approaches towards economic and financial news production in the UK. *Journalism, 7*, 433–452.

Druckman, J. N. (2005). Media matter: How newspapers and television news cover campaigns and influence voters. *Political Communication, 22*, 463–481.

Duch, R. M., & Stevenson, R. T. (2008). *The economic vote: How political and economic institutions condition election results*. Cambridge, UK: Cambridge University Press.

Dyck, A., & Zingales, L. (2003). *The bubble and the media*. In P. Cornelius & B. Kogut (eds.), *Corporate Governance and Capital Flows in a Global Economy* (pp. 83–104). New York: Oxford University Press.

Eilders, C. (2002). Conflict and consonance in media opinion: Political positions of five German quality newspapers. *European Journal of Communication, 17*, 25–63.

Einwiller, S. A., Carroll, C. E., & Korn, K. (2010). Under what conditions do the news media influence corporate reputation? The roles of media dependency and need for orientation. *Corporate Reputation Review, 12*, 299–315.

Entman, R. M. (1993). Framing: Toward clarification of a fractured paradigm. *Journal of Communication, 43*, 51–58.

Feezell, J. T. (2018). Agenda setting through social media: The importance of incidental news exposure and social filtering in the digital era. *Political Research Quarterly, 71*(2), 482–494.

Ferree, M. M., Gamson, W. A., Gerhards, J., & Rucht, D. (2002). Four models of the public sphere in modern democracies. *Theory and Society, 31*, 289–324.

Fogarty, B. J. (2005). Determining economic news coverage. *International Journal of Public Opinion Research, 17*, 149–172.

Fournier, P., Soroka, S., & Nir, L. (2020). Negativity biases and poiitical Ideology: A comparative test across 17 countries. *American Political Science Review, 114*(3), 775–791.

Fox, J. R., Koloen, G., & Sahin, V. M. S. (2007). No joke: A comparison of substance in the Dily Show with Jon Stewart and broadcast network television coverage of the 2004 presidential election campaign. *Journal of Broadcasting & Electronic Media, 51*, 213–227.

Galtung, J., & Ruge, M. H. (1965). The structure of foreign news: The presentation of the Congo, Cuba and Cyprus crises in four Norwegian newspapers. *Journal of Peace Research, 2*, 64–9.

Gattermann, K., & De Vreese, C. H. (2017). The role of candidate evaluations in the 2014 European Parliament elections: Towards the personalization of voting behaviour? *European Union Politics, 18*, 447–468.

Geiß, S., & Schäfer, S. (2017). Any publicity or good publicity? A competitive test of visibility-and tonality-based media effects on voting behavior. *Political Communication, 34*, 444–467.

Gleason, B. (2013). #Occupy Wall Street: Exploring informal learning about a social movement on twitter. *American Behavioral Scientist, 57*, 966–982.

Goidel, R. K., & Langley, R. E. (1995). Media coverage of the economy and aggregate economic evaluations: Uncovering evidence of indirect media effects. *Political Research Quarterly, 48*, 313–328.

Graf-Vlachy, L., Oliver, A.G., Banfield, R., König, A., & Bundy, J. (2019). Media coverage of firms: Background, integration, and directions for future research. *Journal of Management, 46*, 36–69. http://doi.org/1.1177 /0149206319864155

Hagen, L. M. (2005). *Konjunkturnachrichten, Konjunkturklima und Konjunktur. Wie sich die Wirtschaftsberichterstattung der Massenmedien, Stimmungen der Bevölkerung und die aktuelle Wirtschaftslage wechselseitig beeinflussen. Eine transaktionale Analyse*. Köln: Halem.

Haigh, M. M., & Heresco, A. (2010). Late-night Iraq: Monologue joke content and tone from 2003 to 2007. *Mass Communication and Society, 13*, 157–173.

Harcup, T., & O'Neill, D. (2001). What is news? Galtung and Ruge revisited. *Journalism Studies, 2*, 261–28.

Hardy, B. W., Gottfried, J. A., Winneg, K. M., & Jamieson, K. H. (2014). Stephen Colbert's civics lesson: How Colbert super PAC taught viewers about campaign finance. *Mass Communication and Society, 17*, 329–353.

Harrington, D. E. (1989). Economic news on television: The determinants of coverage. *Public Opinion Quarterly, 53*, 17–4.

Hart, R. P., & Hartelius, E. J. (2007). The political sins of Jon Stewart. *Critical Studies in Media Communication, 24*, 263–272.

Hester, J. B., & Gibson, R. (2003). The economy and second-level agenda-setting: A time-series analysis of economic news and public opinion about the economy. *Journalism and Mass Communication Quarterly, 80*, 73–79.

Hetherington, M. J. (1996). The media's role in forming voters' national economic evaluations in 1992. *American Journal of Political Science, 40*, 372–395.

Holbert, R. L. (2013). Developing a normative approach to political satire: An empirical perspective. *International Journal of Communication, 7*, 305–323.

Hollanders, D., & Vliegenthart, R. (2011). The influence of negative newspaper coverage on consumer confidence: The Dutch case. *Journal of Economic Psychology, 32*, 367–373.

Hughes, D. J., Rowe, M., Batey, M., & Lee, A. (2012). A tale of two sites: Twitter vs. Facebook and the personality predictors of social media usage. *Computers in Human Behavior, 28*, 561–569. http://doi.org/1.1016/j .chb.2011.11.001

Hwong, Y., Oliver, C., Van Kranendonk, M., Sammut, C., & Seroussi, Y. (2017). What makes you tick? The psychology of social media engagement in space science communication. *Computers in Human Behavior, 68*, 480–492.

Jerit, J., Barabas, J., & Bolsen, T. (2006). Citizens, knowledge, and the information environment. *American Journal of Political Science, 50*, 266–282.

John, P., & Jennings, W. (2010). Punctuations and turning points in British politics: The policy agenda of the Queen's Speech, 1940–2005. *British Journal of Political Science*, 40, 561-586.

Jonkman, J.G.F., Boukes, M., & Vliegenthart, R. (2020). When do media matter most? A study on the relationship between negative economic news and consumer confidence across the twenty-eight EU states. *The International Journal of Press/Politics, 25*, 76–95.

Jonkman, J. G. F., Boukes, M., Vliegenthart, R., & Verhoeven, P. (2020). Buffering negative news: Individual-level effects of company visibility, tone, and pre-existing attitudes on corporate reputation. *Mass Communication and Society*, 23, 272–296.

Jonkman, J. G. F., Trilling, D., Verhoeven, P., & Vliegenthart, R. (2020). To pass or not to pass: How corporate characteristics affect corporate visibility and tone in company news coverage. *Journalism Studies*, 21(1),1–18.

Ju, A., Jeong, S. H., & Chyi, H. I. (2014). Will social media save newspapers? *Journalism Practice, 8*, 1–17.

Ju, Y. (2008). The asymmetry in economic news coverage and its impact on public perception in South Korea. *International Journal of Public Opinion Research, 20*, 237–249.

Kahneman, D., & Tversky, A. (1979). Prospect theory: An analysis of decision under risk. *Econometrica: Journal of the Econometric Society, 47*, 263–291.

Kahneman, D., & Tversky, A. (1982). The psychology of preferences. *Scientific American, 246*, 160–173.

Kalogeropoulos, A., Albæk, E., de Vreese, C. H., & Van Dalen, A. (2015). The predictors of economic sophistication: Media, interpersonal communication and negative economic experiences. *European Journal of Communication*, *30*, 385–403.

Kalogeropoulos, A., Svensson, H. M., Van Dalen, A., de Vreese, C., & Albæk, E. (2015). Are watchdogs doing their business? media coverage of economic news. *Journalism*, *16*, 993–1009.

Kellstedt, P. M., Linn, S., & Hannah, A. L. (2015). The usefulness of consumer sentiment: Assessing construct and measurement. *Public Opinion Quarterly*, *79*, 181–203.

Kepplinger, H. M., & Ehmig, S. C. (2006). Predicting news decisions. *An empirical test of the two-component theory of news selection. Communications*, *31*, 25–43.

Kiousis, S., Popescu, C., & Mitrook, M. (2007). Understanding influence on corporate reputation: An examination of public relations efforts, media coverage, public opinion, and financial performance from an agenda-building and agenda-setting perspective. *Journal of Public Relations Research*, *19*, 147–165.

Kleinnijenhuis, J., Schultz, F., & Oegema, D., & Van Atteveldt, W. (2013). Financial news and market panics in the age of high-frequency sentiment trading algorithms. *Journalism*, 14, 271–291.

Kleinnijenhuis, J., Schultz, F., & Oegema, D. (2015). Frame complexity and the financial crisis: A comparison of the United States, the United Kingdom, and Germany in the period 2007–2012. *Journal of Communication*, *65*, 1–23.

Koivukoski, J., & Ödmark, S. (2020). Producing journalistic news satire: How Nordic satirists negotiate a hybrid genre. *Journalism Studies*, *21*, 731–747.

Kovach, B., & Rosenstiel, T. (2014). *The elements of journalism: What news people should know and the public should expect*. New York: Three Rivers Press.

Kroon, A. C., Kluknavska, A., Vliegenthart, R., & Boomgaarden, H. G. (2016). Victims or perpetrators? Explaining media framing of Roma across Europe. *European Journal of Communication*, *31*, 375–392.

Kroon, A.C., & Van der Meer, T. G. L. A. (2018). Who takes the lead? Investigating the reciprocal relationship between organizational and news agendas. Communication Research. Advance online publication.

Kwak, H., Lee, C., Park, H., & Moon, S. (2010). (2010). What is Twitter, a social network or a news media? Paper presented at the *Proceedings of the 19th International Conference on World Wide Web*, Raleigh (NC). 591–60.

Larcinese, V., Puglisi, R., & Snyder, J.M. (2011). Partisan bias in economic news: Evidence on the agenda-setting behavior of US newspapers. *Journal of Public Economics*, *95*, 1178–1189.

Lee, E., & Oh, S. Y. (2013). Seek and you shall find? How need for orientation moderates knowledge gain from twitter use. *Journal of Communication, 63,* 745–765.

Lee, S., & Xenos, M. (2019). Social distraction? Social media use and political knowledge in two U.S. presidential elections. *Computers in Human Behavior, 90,* 18–25.

Lengauer, G., Esser, F., & Berganza, R. (2012). Negativity in political news: A review of concepts, operationalizations and key findings. *Journalism, 13,* 179–202.

Lenz, G. S. (2009). Learning and opinion change, not priming: Reconsidering the priming hypothesis. *American Journal of Political Science, 53,* 821–837.

Levendusky, M. S. (2013). Why do partisan media polarize viewers?. *American Journal of Political Science, 57,* 611–623.

Lewis-Beck, M. S., & Paldam, M. (2000). Economic voting: An introduction. *Electoral Studies, 19,* 113–121.

Lewis-Beck, M. S., & Stegmaier, M. (2000). Economic determinants of electoral outcomes. *Annual Review of Political Science, 3,* 183–219.

Loges, W. E., & Ball-Rokeach, S. J. (1993). Dependency relations and newspaper readership. *Journalism Quarterly, 70,* 602–614.

Ludvigson, S. C. (2004). Consumer confidence and consumer spending. *The Journal of Economic Perspectives, 18,* 29–5.

Manning, P. (2013). Financial journalism, news sources, and the banking crisis. *Journalism, 14,* 173–189.

Matsusaka, J. G., & Sbordone, A. M. (1995). Consumer confidence and economic fluctuations. *Economic Inquiry,* 33(2), 296–318.

Matthes, J., & Rauchfleisch, A. (2013). The Swiss "Tina Fey effect." *Communication Quarterly, 61,* 596–614.

McCombs, M. (2005). A look at agenda-setting: Past, present and future. *Journalism Studies, 6,* 543–557.

McCombs, M. E., & Shaw, D. L. (1972). The agenda-setting function of mass media. *Public Opinion Quarterly, 36,* 176–187.

Meijer, M. M., & Kleinnijenhuis J. (2006a). Issue news and corporate reputation: Applying the theories of agenda setting and issue ownership in the field of business communication. *Journal of Communication, 56,* 543–559.

Meijer, M. M., & Kleinnijenhuis J. (2006b). News and corporate reputation: Empirical findings from the Netherlands. *Public Relations Review, 32,* 341–348.

Melenhorst, L. (2015). The media's role in lawmaking: A case study analysis. *The International Journal of Press/Politics,* 20(3), 297–316.

Mindich, D. T. Z. (2005). *Tuned out: Why Americans under 40 don't follow the news*. New York: Oxford University Press.

Morton, T. A., & Duck, J. M. (2001). Communication and health beliefs: Mass and interpersonal influences on perceptions of risk to self and others. *Communication Research, 28*, 602–626.

Müller, P., Schneiders, P., & Schäfer, S. (2016). Appetizer or main dish? Explaining the use of Facebook news posts as a substitute for other news sources. *Computers in Human Behavior, 65*, 431–441.

Mutz, D. C. (1992). Mass media and the depoliticization of personal experience. *American Journal of Political Science, 36*, 483–508.

Mutz, D. C. (1998). *Impersonal influence: How perceptions of mass collectives affect political attitudes*. Cambridge, UK: Cambridge University Press.

Nguyen, V. H., & Claus, E. (2013). Good news, bad news, consumer sentiment and consumption behavior. *Journal of Economic Psychology, 39*, 426–438.

Nieuwenhuis, I. (2018). Televisual satire in the age of glocalization: The case of zondag met lubach. *VIEW Journal of European Television History and Culture, 7*, 69–79.

Nitsch, C., & Lichtenstein, D. (2019). Satirizing international crises: The depiction of the Ukraine, Greek debt, and migration crises in political satire. *Studies in Communication Sciences, 19*, 85–103.

Oeldorf-Hirsch, A. (2018). The role of engagement in learning from active and incidental news exposure on social media. *Mass Communication and Society, 21*, 225–247.

Ohira, H., Winton, W. M., & Oyama, M. (1998). Effects of stimulus valence on recognition memory and endogenous eyeblinks: Further evidence for positive-negative asymmetry. *Personality and Social Psychology Bulletin, 24*, 986–993.

Pallas, J., Strannegård, L., & Jonsson, S. (eds.). (2014). *Organizations and the media: Organizing in a mediatized world*. London: Routledge.

Postman, N. (1986). *Amusing ourselves to death: Public discourse in the age of show business*. London: Heinemann.

Prior, M. (2007). *Post-broadcast democracy: How media choice increases inequality in political involvement and polarizes elections*. New York: Cambridge University Press.

Richey, M. H., Koenigs, R. J., Richey, H. W., & Fortin, R. (1975). Negative salience in impressions of character: Effects of unequal proportions of positive and negative information. *The Journal of Social Psychology, 97*, 233–241.

Robinson-Whelen, S., Kim, C., MacCallum, R. C., & Kiecolt-Glaser, J. K. (1997). Distinguishing optimism from pessimism in older adults: Is it more important to be optimistic or not to be pessimistic? *Journal of Personality and Social Psychology, 73*, 1345–1353.

Sanders, D. (2000). The real economy and the perceived economy in popularity functions: How much do voters need to know? A study of British data, 1974–97. *Electoral Studies, 19*, 275–294.

Scherer, A. G., Palazzo, G., & Matten, D. (2014). The business firm as a political actor: A new theory of the firm for a globalized world. *Business & Society, 53*(2), 143–156.

Scheufele, D. A., & Tewksbury, D. (2007). Framing, agenda setting, and priming: The evolution of three media effects models. *Journal of Communication, 57*, 9–2.

Schiffrin, A. (2015). The press and the financial crisis: A review of the literature. *Sociology Compass, 9*, 639–653.

Schuck, A. R., Vliegenthart, R., & De Vreese, C. H. (2016). Matching theory and data: Why combining media content with survey data matters. *British Journal of Political Science, 46*(1), 205–213.

Sciarini, P., Tresch, A., & Vliegenthart, R. (2020). Political agenda-setting and-building in small consensus democracies: Relationships between media and parliament in the Netherlands and Switzerland. *The Agenda Setting Journal, 4*, 109–134.

Sevenans, J., & Vliegenthart, R. (2016). Political agenda-setting in Belgium and the Netherlands: The moderating role of conflict framing. *Journalism & Mass Communication Quarterly, 93*, 187–203.

Sheafer, T. (2007). How to evaluate it: The role of story-evaluative tone in agenda setting and priming. *Journal of Communication, 57*, 21–39.

Shehata, A., & Strömbäck, J. (2018). Learning political news from social media: Network media logic and current affairs news learning in a high-choice media environment. Communication Research. Advance online publication.

Shehata, A., Hopmann, D. N., Nord, L., & Höijer, J. (2015). Television channel content profiles and differential knowledge growth: A test of the inadvertent learning hypothesis using panel data. *Political Communication, 32*, 377–395.

Sherif, M., & Sherif, C. W. (1967). Attitude as the individual's own categories: The social judgment-involvement approach to attitude and attitude change. In C.W. Sherif & M. Sherif (eds.), *Attitude, ego-involvement, and change* (pp. 105–139). New York: Wiley.

Skovsgaard, M., & Andersen, K. (2020). Conceptualizing news avoidance: Towards a shared understanding of different causes and potential solutions. *Journalism Studies, 21*, 459–476.

Snow, D. A., Vliegenthart, R., & Corrigall-Brown, C. (2007). Framing the French riots: A comparative study of frame variation. *Social Forces, 86,* 385–415.

Sohn, Y. J., & Lariscy, R. W. (2015). A "buffer" or "boomerang?" The role of corporate reputation in bad times. *Communication Research, 42,* 237–259.

Soroka, S. N. (2002). Issue attributes and agenda-setting by media, the public, and policymakers in Canada. *International Journal of Public Opinion Research, 14,* 264–285.

Soroka, S. N. (2006). Good news and bad news: Asymmetric responses to economic information. *Journal of Politics, 68,* 372–385.

Soroka, S. N. (2012). The gatekeeping function: Distributions of information in media and the real world. *Journal of Politics, 74,* 514–528.

Soroka, S. N. (2014). *Negativity in democratic politics.* New York: Cambridge University Press.

Soroka, S. N., Stecula, D. A., & Wlezien, C. (2015). It's (change in) the (future) economy, stupid: Economic indicators, the media, and public opinion. *American Journal of Political Science, 59,* 457–474.

Soroka, S., Daku, M., Hiaeshutter-Rice, D., Guggenheim, L., & Pasek, J. (2018). Negativity and positivity biases in economic news coverage: Traditional versus social media. *Communication Research, 45,* 1078–1098.

Staab, J. F. (1990). The role of news factors in news selection: A theoretical reconsideration. *European Journal of Communication, 5,* 423–443.

Strauß, N. (2019). Financial journalism in the post-crisis era. *Journalism, 20:* 274–291.

Strömbäck, J. (2005). In search of a standard: Four models of democracy and their normative implications for journalism. *Journalism Studies, 6,* 331–345.

Stroud, N. J. (2010). Polarization and partisan selective exposure. *Journal of Communication, 60,* 556–576.

Svensson, H. M., Albæk, E., van Dalen, A., & De Vreese, C. H. (2017). The impact of ambiguous economic news on uncertainty and consumer confidence. *European Journal of Communication, 32,* 85–99.

Taber, C. S., & Lodge, M. (2006). Motivated skepticism in the evaluation of political beliefs. *American Journal of Political Science, 50,* 755–769.

Tambini, D. (2010). What are financial journalists for? *Journalism Studies, 11,* 158–174.

Thelwall, M., Buckley, K., & Paltoglou, G. (2013). Sentiment strength detection for the social web. *International Review of Research in Open and Distance Learning, 14,* 90–103.

Thelwall, M., Buckley, K., Paltoglou, G., Cai, D., & Kappas, A. (2010). Sentiment strength detection in short informal text. *Journal of the American Society for Information Science and Technology*, 61, 2544–2558.

Thesen, G. (2013). When good news is scarce and bad news is good: Government responsibilities and opposition possibilities in political agenda-setting. *European Journal of Political Research*, *52*, 364–389.

Tichenor, P. J., Donohue, G. A., & Olien, C. N. (1970). Mass media flow and differential growth in knowledge. *Public Opinion Quarterly*, *34*, 159–17.

Tsfati, Y., & Cappella, J. N. (2003). Do people watch what they do not trust? *Communication Research*, *30*, 504–529.

Usher, N. (2017). Making business news: A production analysis of *The New York Times*. *International Journal of Communication*, 11: 363–382.

Van Aelst, P., & Vliegenthart, R. (2014). Studying the tango: An analysis of parliamentary questions and press coverage in the Netherlands. *Journalism Studies*, *15*, 392–41.

Van Dalen, A., de Vreese, C., & Albæk, E. (2017). Economic news through the magnifying glass. *Journalism Studies*, *18*, 890–909.

Van Dalen, A., Svensson, H., Kalogeropoulos, A., Albæk, E., & De Vreese, C. H. (2018). *Economic news: informing the inattentive audience*. Routledge.

Van der Meer, T. G. L. A., Verhoeven, P., Beentjes, H., & Vliegenthart, R. (2014). When frames align: The interplay between PR, news media, and the public in times of crisis. *Public Relations Review*, *40*, 751–761.

Van der Pas, D. J., van der Brug, W., & Vliegenthart, R. (2017). Political parallelism in media and political agenda-setting. *Political Communication*, *34*, 491–51.

Verhoeven, P. (2009). Corporate actors in Western European television news. *Public Relations Review*, *35*, 297–30.

Vliegenthart, R., & Damstra, A. (2019). Parliamentary questions, newspaper coverage, and consumer confidence in times of crisis: A cross-national comparison. *Political Communication*, *36*, 17–35.

Vliegenthart, R., & Mena Montes, N. (2014). How political and media system characteristics moderate interactions between newspapers and parliaments: Economic crisis attention in Spain and the Netherlands. *International Journal of Press/Politics*, *19*, 318–339.

Vliegenthart, R., & Walgrave, S. (2011). Content matters: The dynamics of parliamentary questioning in Belgium and Denmark. *Comparative Political Studies*, *44*, 1031–1059.

Vliegenthart, R., Walgrave, S., Baumgartner, F. R., et al. (2016). Do the media set the parliamentary agenda? A comparative study in seven countries. *European Journal of Political Research, 55*, 283–301.

Vogler, D., & Eisenegger, M. (2020). CSR communication, corporate reputation, and the role of the news media as an agenda-setter in the digital age. Business & Society. Advance online publication.

Walgrave, S., & Van Aelst, P. (2006). The contingency of the mass media's political agenda setting power: Toward a preliminary theory. *Journal of Communication, 56*, 88–109.

Wang, S. (2017, December 18). How much news makes it into people's Facebook feeds? Our experiment suggests not much. *NiemanLab.* www .niemanlab.org/2017/12/how-much-news-makes-it-into-peoples-facebook-feeds-our-experiment-suggests-not-much/.

Wu, H. D., Stevenson, R. L., Chen, H. C., & Güner, Z. N. (2002). The conditioned impact of recession news: A time-series analysis of economic communication in the United States, 1987–1996. *International Journal of Public Opinion Research, 14*, 19–36.

Yoo, S. W., & Gil de Zúñiga, H. (2014). Connecting blog, twitter and facebook use with gaps in knowledge and participation. *Communication & Society, 27*, 33–48.

Young, D. G., & Hoffman, L. (2012). Acquisition of current-events knowledge from political satire programming: An experimental approach. *Atlantic Journal of Communication, 20*(5), 290–304.

Zhang, X. (2016). Measuring media reputation: A test of the construct validity and predictive power of seven measures. *Journalism & Mass Communication Quarterly, 93*, 884–905.

Zhang, X. (2018). Estimating the weights of media tonalities in the measurement of media coverage of corporations. *Communication Research, 45*, 987–1011.

Zucker, H.G. (1978). The variable nature of news media influence. *Annals of the International Communication Association, 2*, 225–24.

Cambridge Elements

Politics and Communication

Stuart Soroka
University of Michigan
Stuart Soroka is the Michael W. Traugott Collegiate Professor of Communication and Media & Political Science, and Research Professor in the Center for Political Studies at the Institute for Social Research, University of Michigan. His research focuses on political communication, the sources and/or structure of public preferences for policy, and the relationships between public policy, public opinion, and mass media. His books include *Negativity in Democratic Politics* (2014) and *Degrees of Democracy* (with Christopher Wlezien, 2010), both with Cambridge University Press.

About the Series
Cambridge Elements in Politics and Communication publishes research focused on the intersection of media, technology, and politics. The series emphasizes forward-looking reviews of the field, path-breaking theoretical and methodological innovations, and the timely application of social-scientific theory and methods to current developments in politics and communication around the world.

Cambridge Elements $^{\equiv}$

Politics and Communication

Elements in the Series

A full series listing is available at: www.cambridge.org/EPCM

Printed in the United States
by Baker & Taylor Publisher Services